garden
design

garden
design

p

This is a Parragon Book
First published in 2002

Parragon
Queen Street House
4 Queen Street
Bath BA1 1HE, UK
Copyright © Parragon 2002

ISBN: 0-75257-441-8

A CIP data record for this book is available from the British Library.

Created and produced by
Foundry Design and Production

Acknowledgements
Illustrations: Kate Simunek
Special photography: Andrew Newton-Cox

Printed in China

CONTENTS

❦

INTRODUCTION

❦

Planning your garden from the very beginning is vital, and helps you get exactly what you want. Whether you desire a romantic retreat or a formal Japanese garden, this book will show you how to plan, plant, and maintain your chosen scheme. All you need is a little time and patience, and your gardening dreams will be fulfilled.

✿

Approaching your garden with a view to changing it can be intimidating. Many gardeners are put off by the seemingly vast amount of knowledge that is needed to plan and maintain any kind of plot – be it large or small. This book shows you that you don't need to be an expert to get the kind of garden that you want. Any garden can be tailored to suit individual tastes and, as your confidence grows, so will your expertise and knowledge.

✿

The basic principles of garden planning and design are introduced here. The introductory sections deal with the elements of garden planning that you cannot ignore, such as position, aspect and soil type. Then the book moves on to actually getting to work and making the necessary changes. The final section deals with garden styles, and lists many different kinds of garden that you could emulate – all with practical planting information and tips.

✿

So, whether you're an amateur gardener who wants to turn a small garden into a contemporary patio, or someone slightly more expert who wants to transform a cottage garden with a traditional planting scheme, then this book will guide you every step of the way.

GARDEN PLANNING

Your ideal garden might seem far out of reach and unattainable. Don't worry – take your time. A garden can wait and so can you.

❁

The first step is deciding what you want and the second is turning it into reality. A garden is a very personal thing and everybody wants something different.

❁

Do not be afraid to play around with ideas; even the most experienced professional designers will not come up with the correct solution in an afternoon.

❁

Mistakes will be made – and indeed are often made by professionals, too – but you can always change things. Any garden is a living, growing entity; it can always be adjusted.

YOU AND YOUR GARDEN

There are two aspects to the initial decision making.
One is to think about your ideal garden – the garden you see in your
day-dreams, the equivalent to the Middle Eastern paradise garden.
What are your secret dreams for this small patch of land? The other is
to think about the practical aspects, such as providing storage for garden
tools and a place to dry the washing. It is useful to make a checklist of
what you require. Here are some possible ideas for your dream garden.

CHECKLIST FOR YOUR 'IDEAL' GARDEN

ENTERTAINING can be one of the most enjoyable uses of a garden. A generous vine-covered patio, a barbecue area or a croquet lawn may be your dream. If you cannot incorporate all these features, some of them should certainly be possibilities. Other than entertaining, consider the following requirements, too.

Privacy and peace

❀ For some people the most important requirement of a garden is to create a private outdoor space. A tall hedge or trellis with climbers may not cut out all sounds but it will certainly help you to be less aware of them and will effectively separate you from your neighbours. A romantic arbour with a comfortable seat within the garden, surrounded by rambling roses, honeysuckle and clematis, can provide a secluded, peaceful place in which to relax and enjoy the garden.

BELOW: *The romantic arbour, par excellence. This one would fit well in a small garden with its neat shape and simple wooden bench, and its surrounding of white roses and scented lavender.*

❀ Not everyone finds peace the ideal, however. You may prefer to sit in your small front garden and watch the world go by. Here, a hedge would get in the way, so you might prefer a paved area with pots of flowering plants and perhaps two larger shrubs to give the garden an entrance.

LEFT: *A herb border can be an attractive feature of a garden. This one has contrasting leaf sizes as well as scent and colour.*

Water

❀ Water has a refreshing quality in any garden. Whether you want a quiet, still pool that will reflect the sky or take on an almost black mysteriousness, or whether you prefer the lively gurgle of a fountain or cascade, some form of water feature will give the garden an added dimension. Pools do not need to take up much space; a tiny pool with a miniature jet in a lined barrel on the patio, or a small basin with a narrow jet of water pouring into it from a lion's head on the wall can be effective. Place your water feature where you will enjoy it most, so that you can hear it without straining or gaze into it from a comfortable chair. You may even want a swimming pool and that may not be an impossibility in a moderately large garden.

Colour

❀ The green of foliage on its own can create a garden with a great sense of unity. At the same time, because there are so many different shades of green, and because leaves come in different shapes, rustle in different ways and catch the light differently, a foliage garden is endlessly interesting, without any extra colour.

❀ However, many people like bright colours and this is where a knowledge of plants, when they flower and where they will flower best, can be very helpful.

❀ To begin with, it is a good idea to add annuals or bedding plants where there are gaps, but as you become more knowledgeable you will find you like to experiment with all sorts of different colour and plant combinations.

Scent

❀ This is one of the most evocative aspects of a garden. It is worth trying to introduce as many scented plants as possible. In general, the scent from plants is most noticeable in the evening, so think of putting plants such as honeysuckles, scented roses and philadelphus where you are most likely to be sitting with an evening drink. Remember that some scents are more pleasing than others – privet, for example, has a rather overbearing scent, even during the day. Most of the scented flowers are also those that attract wildlife, and are therefore worth planting for that reason alone.

CHECKLIST OF GARDEN FEATURES

Before starting on your design, it is useful to make a list of all the requirements for your ideal garden. Some of these will be necessities, while you may have to compromise on others. Use this checklist at the planning stage.

BARBECUE	☐
BIRD BATH	☐
COMPOST HEAP	☐
DUSTBIN AREA	☐
GARAGE	☐
GRAVELLED AREA	☐
GREENHOUSE	☐
HERB GARDEN	☐
HERBACEOUS BORDER	☐
LAWN	☐
PATIO	☐
PERGOLA	☐
PLAY AREA	☐
POND	☐
RAISED FLOWER-BED	☐
SANDPIT	☐
SHRUB BORDER	☐
SUMMERHOUSE	☐
SUNDIAL	☐
TERRACED AREA	☐
TOOL SHED	☐
VEGETABLE PLOT	☐

CHECKLIST FOR PRACTICALITIES IN YOUR GARDEN

HAVING pinned down your emotional feelings about the garden and what would make it your personal ideal, you then have to take a close look at the practical aspects. Again, it is sensible to make a checklist, including all the things you need for the garden to make it function well for you. When finished, you will have to make compromises, but you will have the basis for dovetailing the practical with the ideal for a result that you can really savour and enjoy. Below are some possible ideas for your practical checklist.

Somewhere to sit

❀ It is useful to have a patio near the house, where food and drink can be carried in and out. However, if the sun shines best in another part of the garden at the time when you usually want to sit out, it would be better to make a patio there. It may even be a good idea to have two sitting areas, one for the sun in the morning and another that will catch the evening sun. Single seats can be dotted around in various places where they will be inviting at different times of day.

Sunbathing area

❀ This needs to be a hot spot, where the sun shines for most of the day. It also needs to be secluded. In a small garden the patio near the house is often the best place. Remember that if you grow tall plants or climbers to screen off neighbours, they may also screen the sun.

ABOVE: *Attractive in its own right, this miniature log cabin makes a playing area that will entertain young children for many hours.*

Somewhere to play

❀ Children may take up the whole garden for their play, in which case all you can hope to do is plant sturdy but decorative shrubs around the edges and wait until the children are older before planning a more subtle garden. If your garden is big enough and you can provide an interesting enough play area, you may get children to concentrate on that area, leaving at least a little space in the garden for your own pursuits.

❀ A climbing frame and swing can keep children happy for hours. Put plenty of bark underneath to cushion any falls. For younger children it may be more sensible to keep the play area near the house where you can keep an eye on them. A sandpit or a small pool can be located near the garden door and covered when not in use.

❀ By the time children go to school, they often become interested in gardening themselves. Giving them a little plot of their own with sturdy, quick-growing plants and practical garden tools can encourage them to enjoy the garden in all sorts of ways.

Garden buildings

❀ Every garden needs a storage area of some kind. A large shed can be the answer but if you are short of space, there are many smaller sheds available. Using dual-purpose seating/storage units means you do not have to give up so much of the garden.

LEFT: *A secluded paved area offers peaceful shade for a quiet retreat. The planting is also subdued – mainly anemones and grasses.*

❀ A garden room can be something as slight as an open-sided summer-house or as sturdy as an insulated workroom, as decorative as a Swiss chalet or as basic as a garden shed with windows. If it will be very much part of the 'viewed' garden, a decorative shed may be best, but remember that modern paints can cheer up most buildings and planting can camouflage them.

Somewhere to grow and propagate

❀ A vegetable plot need not take up too much space and can be given a small, sunny corner of its own, perhaps behind a hedge or fence or through a flower-covered arch. Composting goes with food production. It is a way of using up waste material usefully and of getting rid of annual weeds and grass clippings. However, you should be aware that no small garden will be able to provide enough compost for its own requirements. You will have to supplement any you make with organic matter from elsewhere.

❀ A greenhouse is a good idea only if you are really going to have time to use, water, clean and generally care for it. Cold frames and cloches may be enough for beginners or somebody who has little time.

ABOVE: *This neat rubbish-bin cupboard takes up little space, has a waterproof roof and is stained an attractive dark green so that it blends in well with the garden.*

Accommodating wheelchair gardeners

❀ Remember that if you are making allowances for wheelchairs, you must provide not only paths wide enough for the wheelchair to negotiate but also turning spaces. Gravel is difficult for wheelchairs but bricks or paving are ideal. Raised beds can make gardening easier and more fun, while raised pools and water channels are more interesting, too.

BELOW: *This hexagonal summerhouse adds a contemporary touch to the garden, with its cheerful blue-painted woodwork.*

GETTING TO KNOW
YOUR GARDEN

❦

You have made checklists of your own needs and it is now time
to assess the plot itself. There is a tremendous amount you need
to know before you can confidently begin to design and, unlike
a room within the house, the garden will repay you if you have
patience and live with it for a year before making any drastic changes.

WHAT TO LOOK FOR

WHATEVER time of year you move into your new
home, give yourself 12 months to observe the
garden. It will almost certainly surprise you with
unsuspected spring bulbs, dead-looking twigs that turn
into splendid clematis or herbaceous plants appearing
seemingly from nowhere.

❀ Use a notebook to jot down the interesting things
that happen over the year, particularly those that
are worth keeping.

❀ Look at the garden from the windows of the house
and note where views are blocked or eyesores are
open to view.

❀ Note where the sun shines for most of the day, which
part of the garden gets sun in the morning only and
which only in the afternoon. Note how the garden
behaves in different weather, what suffers if there is
a drought and what gets knocked flat in strong winds.
Note whether noise comes from a particular quarter.

ABOVE: *Cheerful little hardy cyclamen can brighten up the garden in autumn
or winter, depending on which species you choose, they cover the bare ground
under trees.*

ABOVE: *Spring in a woodland garden with the heavenly blue of the
Himalayan blue poppy (Meconopsis betonicifolia) and a speckling
of varnished yellow buttercups.*

❀ Note if there is any wildlife. Lots of insects and worms mean the garden is fertile and plants should grow well. A complete lack of insect life – except, perhaps, white-fly and greenfly – means the soil badly needs air and compost or other organic matter. If you displace any frogs and toads while clearing out moist patches around drains, try to provide other sources of water because these are among the gardener's friends.

In spring

❀ Notice what bulbs come up that you didn't know about. Are they pretty and in the right place? Are there some missing that you would like to have? Snowdrops are an absolute blessing in the early spring garden and if they feel at home will multiply quickly. Are there any spring-flowering shrubs? Do not remove any dead-looking stalks at this stage. Many clematis and hardy hibiscus, for example, look like pieces of old sticks or string until they start to put out surprisingly sturdy leaves and buds early in the summer.

In summer

❀ Look for dull shrubs that are not pulling their weight; branches of trees that have grown too large and are cutting out necessary light. Few people realise how much light is excluded by overgrown trees and how this stunts the growth of other plants in the garden. Look for

unexpected perennials poking through the soil – are they too leggy, or riddled with perennial weeds? Or are they a delightful surprise? Summer bulbs such as alliums and lilies may appear, too.

In autumn

❀ Watch for leaves that turn a wonderful colour or for brightly coloured berries that liven up the shorter days. Pyracanthas, so often used as hedging plants, are good 'security' shrubs because of their thorns but they also have pretty white flowers and spectacular berries in autumn. Bulbs often come up with surprises: look for autumn crocuses and, in later summer, tiny hardy cyclamen under trees. If you do not find these, put them on your wish list of plants. They are all exquisite.

In winter

❀ Look at the framework of the garden. Does it still look good when the flowers are all over? Are there any deciduous trees? If so, do they mean the garden looks rather bare, or do you like the feeling of light that this gives for a few months? Remember that spring bulbs and early flowers can grow under deciduous trees because of the light they receive early in the year, whereas many will not thrive under evergreens.

Front gardens

❀ In the front garden have a look at any rubbish bins. Are they well concealed behind a wall or a clipped hedge? Could they be better placed? Do people throw drink cans and crisp bags into the garden? A closely clipped, prickly evergreen hedge might stop this happening.

ABOVE: The tall bearded iris is a late spring plant. This yellow and mauve one catches the spring sunlight and is seen here growing in a wild garden designed for low maintenance.

ABOVE: This garden backs on to a field, which allows the snow-covered trees at its perimeter to catch the late evening sun with a warm glow.

INTERIM ACTION

ALTHOUGH it is best not to do too much planting or redesigning during the first year in a garden, there is plenty to be getting on with in the meantime.

Clear rubble and rubbish

❀ Many gardens have areas where the builders have tipped rubble rather than carry it to the dump. It is important that this is removed because bits of brick and cement are not conducive to growing things and often contain lime, which many plants do not like. If you have to carry rubble through the house, try to get old builders' bags, which are large, very tough and will shed less dust as you pass through. If the garden contains electrical items such as a microwave oven or refrigerator, it is usually possible to call the local authority and ask for them to be removed.

Clear bramble and weed patches

❀ If a patch of ground is infested with troublesome weeds like brambles, ground elder, nettles or the infamous Japanese knotweed, take the opportunity to clear it now. There is no point in cosseting any plant that may be growing among them. It is best to get rid of everything and start again.

❀ Nettles have shallow roots and it is usually possible to pull or dig them out. Brambles can be killed with brushwood killer but ground elder and Japanese knotweed are weeds of a tougher sort. It is best to use glyphosate in spring, when they are growing most vigorously, because the chemical runs through their sap and down into their roots. With both weeds you will

BELOW: *Do not be afraid to prune. The annual cutting back of these trees has encouraged new shoots and produced a wonderful display of contrasting colour without taking over the whole garden.*

probably have to give a second application when they come into vigorous growth again in late summer. To be on the safe side, you should apply the herbicide again the following spring. The chemical is no longer active when it reaches the soil, so if you are sure you have scotched the weed, you can plant when you want.

Prune trees

❀ Most people are reluctant at first to have trees pruned but, in fact, once pruned, they will spring into growth better than before, and letting light into the garden is absolutely essential if you want to grow healthy plants. However, trees may be protected and in some areas all trees are protected so you need to find out whether you need permission before you go ahead. You should check that the arborist is fully insured before you allow him or her to go up your tree and that the removal of all branches is part of the deal.

Mend fences and walls

❀ Unless you think you might alter the existing fences and walls, this is a good time to get them mended or replaced. Once you have done any planting, it will be difficult to get at fences without damaging the plants. Check that any fences are secure with strong posts and that any trellis is solidly built and firmly fixed. Trellis often has quite a weight to bear if you grow an evergreen clematis or a vigorous climbing rose against it.

Provide temporary colour

❀ Even if the garden surprises you with unexpected treats, a neglected garden is unlikely to provide enough colour during the first summer. But there is plenty of temporary planting you can do to brighten up the garden for one season. Mallow plants are not expensive and one plant will grow to 2 m (7 ft) in a year and be covered with open pink flowers, giving a good display throughout summer and autumn.

❀ You can let yourself go with plants and containers. Pelargoniums will brighten up sunny places, busy Lizzies (*Impatiens*) are happy in light shade and abutilons will create an exotic atmosphere against warm

walls. You can place pots with brightly coloured flowers throughout the garden. Of course, annuals and bedding plants will fill gaps. Petunias, verbenas, *Salvia splendens* and pelargoniums can provide plenty of colour.

Use the time

❀ It is good to use this year to inspect as many other gardens as you can. Look at their layouts, the details of their paths and steps and, of course, their planting. If something intrigues you, take a photograph and make a note of it. It may be useful when you are trying to solve a problem later on.

BELOW: *Containers can provide plenty of interest while you are waiting to tackle your garden. Here, various terracotta pots and a galvanised bin give a brave display of green and mauve that will be attractive all winter.*

SURVEYING THE SITE

Begin by making a site plan. It should be an accurate record of the
boundary of your garden and the main items within it – the house,
existing buildings, trees and ponds. It should show where the ground
rises, where there are steps, which way the garden faces and where
there are eyesores to be concealed or views to be enjoyed. Note on the
plan those areas of the garden in the sun and those in shade. You should
also note the type of soil and whether it is extremely dry, well drained
or boggy, or whether it is dry in summer and soggy in winter.

THE PLAN

IT IS best to do your survey on graph paper, which
helps to get the measurements accurate. Measure the
boundary of the garden first. You should use a 30 m
(100 ft) measuring tape, and you will find measuring
easier with two people to hold the tape.

House

❀ Mark where the house is in relation to the garden,
and its size and distance from the boundaries. Show
the position of the ground floor windows and doors
and make sure you indicate which side faces north.

ABOVE: *This pastel-painted seaside home needs plants that are able to
withstand the salt-laden breezes. Ceanothus and wisteria do well, and there
is a shelter belt of hawthorns further down the hill.*

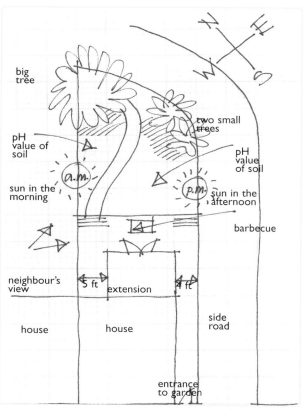

ABOVE: *A rough sketch of your garden need not be a beautiful drawing.
Provided the measurements are correct and more or less in scale, you can sketch
the garden several times, trying out different ideas. Here, the house is shown with
its extension into the garden and its relationship to the road. The north/south
aspect should be shown, as should all big trees, sheds and other structures; you
can try different placings of paths, areas for barbecues and so on.*

LEFT: Terracing a garden is a good way of dealing with steeply rising ground. The terraces can be very attractively planted, with each level offering a different type of garden. It is best to get such a site professionally surveyed.

Shade

❀ Mark areas that are in shadow for most of the day. This may be a good area for a dog kennel or for a play area, although a little sun will be welcome, of course. Areas in deep shadow will require careful planting because only a limited number of plants will thrive in them.

Soil type and drainage

❀ Find out whether your soil type is basically clay, sand or loam. Clay is heavy, difficult to work and clogs into mud that comes indoors on your boots. It warms up slowly in spring but with lots of organic matter added it will become workable and more nutritious than other soils.

❀ Sandy soil is light, easy to work and drains easily, which means that nutrients are likely to drain away, too. Loam is probably the ideal. It is dark and sweet smelling, crumbles in the fingers and holds water well. Very dry soil can be given additives to help it retain water. Draining boggy soil can be expensive. Instead of draining you could create a specialist bog garden where suitable plants will thrive.

❀ An analysis of your soil will tell you whether it is acidic, alkaline or neutral (which is best for most gardens). The pH of a soil – its degree of acidity/alkalinity – is important as some plants require an acidic soil and others require an alkaline one. The pH can range from around 5 (acidic) to 8 (alkaline), 6.5 being neutral and suitable for a great many plants. Soil-testing kits are inexpensive and available from garden centres. Test the soil in several parts of the garden, since the pH may vary within a small area.

Alterations in level

❀ Show where the ground level alters and measure the width of any existing steps. It can be difficult to work out accurately the rise and fall of ground without special equipment. On a difficult site it is best to get a level survey done by a professional but if you do not need complete accuracy, you can use fences, walls and steps for guidance.

Aspect

❀ Mark which way the garden faces. This will enable you to decide on the best positions for seating and play areas, vegetable plots, flower and shrub borders and many other features that need to be either sheltered or sunny.

Trees

❀ Show all existing large trees and indicate where your neighbours' trees cast shade into your garden. If a tree is in the wrong place or has grown too large, consider getting rid of it and replacing it with something more suitable.

ABOVE: The paved area in front of the house has been designed in a semicircular arrangement of bricks leading towards the house. The brick colour blends in well with the roof tiles.

RECOMMENDATIONS AND PRACTICALITIES

YOU have noted on your plan the salient points of the garden as it is, using the notes you made during the first year and the measurements taken during the survey.

You should now be thinking about how you want to alter the garden, what you want to remove and what you want to add. There are a number of practical considerations that will make creating the actual plan easier. For example, it is useful to know that the clearance needed for a swing is 7 m (23 ft).

Remember that everything should be in scale with the house. A very tall house will require a larger patio, taller trees and arches, and larger spaces. A bungalow will need everything on a slightly smaller scale if the garden is not to look pretentious.

Conservatory

❀ It is not good to have a conservatory on the south side of a house where it is too hot most of the time. A better position is the east or west side for sitting, or the north if the important thing is growing plants. As with other structures, a good conservatory will be in keeping with the house. A modern, simple building will suit a modern house, whereas a gothic creation will look fine added to a red brick mansion.

BELOW: *Similar bricks have been used here for both the paving and the wall to give a sense of unity to the design. The paved area is surrounded by a luxurious planting of pinks and purples.*

Steps and paths

❀ Steps should be comfortable to climb up and down. A leisurely scale is right for a garden. They are not like house stairs, which are designed to go up quickly. The slope should not be more than 40° from the horizontal, otherwise steps appear unwelcoming.

❀ The minimum safe riser (the vertical part) for steps in a garden is 100 mm (4 in). If they are shorter, someone might trip on them. The maximum is 200 mm (8 in). The tread should ideally be 300 mm (12 in) deep. A good proportion for garden steps is a 150 mm (6 in) riser with a 375 mm (15 in) tread, although in a small garden that may not always be possible. Steps do take up more room than is generally realised. Six steps, 1.8 m (6 ft) wide with treads 450 mm (18 in) deep, will take up 4.8 sq m (54 sq ft). This could take up a very significant proportion of a small garden.

❀ With stone or brick steps it is best if the tread projects slightly over the riser at the front to create a shadow line. This not only looks good but also helps to define the steps in poor light.

❀ If you are creating a long flight of steps, remember that you will need a 'landing' every 10 or 12 steps, which should be twice as deep as the steps.

❀ Paths can be wide or narrow, as scale or space permits. A wide path allows two people to walk along in conversation but may take up more space than the garden can easily allow. A narrow path will keep your feet dry in wet weather and may be all that is needed.

Pergolas

❀ A pergola is an important garden structure. The design and materials will affect the whole look of the garden. Supporting piers of brick or stone need large solid crossbars to be in scale. Wooden uprights with slender beams make a more elegant construction, suitable for smaller gardens and lighter climbers such as clematis and less vigorous roses.

❀ The height of your pergola is critical. The bar at the top will have something climbing on it, which will make it slightly higher, so 2.4 m (8 ft) is a good height. In a very small garden you could go down to 2 m (7 ft) and in a very large garden up to 2.7 m (9 ft).

❀ With any sort of opening, including arches, the wider and more generous it is, the more welcoming it will be.

Paving

❀ This also has an important structural role in the garden. It should always look good. Paving can be used for anything from patios and parking spaces to paths and steps; in small and urban gardens it can take the place of a lawn.

❀ Natural stone, concrete, brick, tiles, paviours and wood can all be used in different combinations. Do not try to use too many materials at once, however, or you will end up with an uncoordinated result. It is best never to use more than three different materials. This will help to create unity throughout the garden.

❀ Remember to make the patio large enough. You need room not only for a table with chairs tucked in neatly around it, but for people to pull the chairs out and sit in them. Any patio should therefore be at least 3 x 3.5 m (10 x 12 ft).

ABOVE: *A slightly curved flight of gravel and timber steps has wide treads and shallow risers, which give it an unhurried, relaxed quality.*

ABOVE: *Even the smallest space can be packed with interest by the clever use of different media, textures, colours and shapes.*

THE CONCEPT PLAN

This is where you get to fit all your requirements into your actual garden.
You should have decided by now whether you want to bulldoze the
whole garden and start again from scratch, or whether there is enough of
a sensible outline to allow you to work round what you already have.
Consider how you can make the transition from garden to house as smooth
and pleasant as possible. French windows or patio doors are ideal and can
be made secure with double-glazing, laminated glass and good locks. If
you are not able to change the door, you can design the garden so that the
view from the windows is enticing.

EXPERIMENTING WITH IDEAS

MAKE lots of copies of your initial survey sketch and
try out ideas in pencil on these. Decide on the most
important of your requirements and sacrifice the others,
allowing a few generous spaces in your garden rather than
too many slightly mean ones. This will make the garden
less fussy and bitty and ultimately give more pleasure.

ABOVE: *Any ordinary garden shed can become an integral part of the
garden by concealing it with ivy or creeper. Both are used here, with the
creeper turning a bright red in autumn.*

Using photographs

❀ Your plan or 'map' is useful for getting a feeling of
the balance of the different areas within the space,
but will not give you a picture of the three-dimensional
reality of the garden. For this it is useful to look at
your photographs and try out some of your ideas on
them. A good way of doing this is to lay pieces of
tracing paper over them and sketch out different ideas
– the more you do, the better. You will find you begin
to revert to a particular idea. When your ideas begin
to firm up, make a new plan with everything on it that
you want to retain and everything you want to change.

❀ One of the most difficult things is imagining how the
plants will look when they have matured and grown,
particularly trees and shrubs. This is where your
overlay and photographs can help. If you know a shrub
is eventually going to become 2 m (7 ft) tall, you can
see what effect this will have on the garden plan in a
few years' time.

❀ On your initial sketches think of how you can make the
garden more interesting and effective. There are several
ways in which you can entirely change the appearance
of a garden without too much outlay.

Alterations

❀ You might want to move a path nearer to a fence, or
further from it, to provide a wider border, or take it
diagonally across the garden to create two separate
spaces. Diagonal lines across a narrow garden can
make it look wider.

❀ You can move a small shed, instead of getting rid of it,
to a place where it is less obtrusive and can be concealed

behind climbers. Paint can give dull little buildings
a more cheerful look.

Extending

❀ You can continue a straight border around in a curve
to conceal a shed or surround the shed with shrubs.
A greenhouse that is not particularly pretty can also
be surrounded by low-growing shrubs. They cannot be
too tall or they will cut out too much light and things
inside the greenhouse will grow spindly in their
attempts to reach the light.

Enlarging and dividing

❀ You can enlarge an existing patio or make it
circular instead of rectangular; you might want to
make a path wider, to emphasise its direction and
lead people on. Using a tall, sturdy trellis fence to
divide the patio and the garden can give privacy
without completely cutting off the view. This gives
an extra place for growing climbers.

BELOW: *In this garden, the patio has been extended into a pathway with
planted borders to lead people through the garden.*

MORE IDEAS AND POSSIBILITIES

GARDENS are made up of spaces and shapes for various activities; the bits in between are your planting spaces. When you have sketched in the shapes for, say, sitting, paths, shed, pond, play and vegetable garden and you have eliminated the least essential, go through the whole process again until you have spaces that will fit well into your garden.

Thinking ahead

❀ If your basic framework works well, later on you will be able to change how you use it. For example, if you build a brick sandpit, butting on to a brick-edged lawn, as the children grow older, you will be able to exchange sand for water and have a garden pool. A playhouse can be a marvellous place for children to play in. If you have chosen a solid one you can have it insulated and eventually take it over as a retreat or even a serious workroom.

❀ One early decision, especially in a small garden, must be whether you want a lawn or would prefer to have paving. A small lawn can be a refreshing source of green in an urban winter. Some gardeners derive enormous pleasure from mowing a pocket handkerchief of greenery but a very small garden may not have room to store a lawnmower. Moreover, if the lawn is too overshadowed or impoverished, it will just look sparse and sad. In that case, it will be best to have it all up and lay paving slabs or a pattern of bricks or cobbles for a crisp and clean surface, which may better suit the urban environment or the busy working person.

Features beyond the garden

❀ Mark any good views on your plan and lead the eye to them by creating a gap in the hedge or a circular 'window' in a wall. A path leading in that direction and a seat facing the view will encourage people to enjoy it. Similarly, mark any bad views on your plan so that you can conceal your neighbour's rusty swing or ugly shed with trellis and climbers or a well-placed columnar tree.

❀ Make the best use of any attractive trees and tall flowering shrubs in neighbouring gardens. Doing this will not only provide extra colour in your own garden but also help extend the sense of space. Hedges can be cut a little lower to allow a view of a neighbouring blue ceanothus or pink camellia.

ABOVE: *A sense of spaciousness is achieved in a small area by narrow borders along the fencing and several unimposing features including a seat, trellis and central plant arrangements.*

ABOVE: *This miniature lawn will never need mowing, since it is made of camomile. Although only tiny, it provides a welcome touch of fresh green within this charming seating area.*

THINGS TO AVOID

❀ Avoid mixing formal with informal. You lose the sense of harmony that you are aiming for by moving from one to the other. Informal gardens are much more difficult to design than formal ones. The symmetry of a formal garden really designs itself – you can hardly go wrong – whereas the curves and shapes of an informal design require a balance that may not always be obvious.

❀ Avoid mixing different styles. This creates an uncomfortable feeling and diminishes the impact of any one style.

❀ Avoid combining curves and straight edges. Sometimes a circle can be satisfactorily placed within a square but, in general, curves and straight edges are difficult to combine. Try to create generous curves with serpentine paths or borders. These should flow, not wiggle, so that the curves are in wide sweeps rather than worm-like kinks.

A feeling of space

❀ Small gardens can be made to seem much more spacious by designing in diagonals. A path running diagonally from one side of the garden to the other and then back again at an angle will divide the garden into three. The spaces made in this way can be separated by tall or low planting and will make the garden seem larger because the eye cannot see exactly where the garden ends and is intrigued by the planting between.

❀ Arches create a feeling of space by implying that there is more happening beyond them. Arches should always lead to something or the result is disappointment. A small gate under the arch will enhance the feeling of entering into a different domain.

A sense of unity

❀ When you have an idea of what you want, stick with it throughout the whole garden. This will give the garden cohesion and a sense of unity, which is one of the hallmarks of all successful gardens. Decide whether you want the garden to be formal or informal, or asymmetrical with overlapping squares and geometric shapes.

ABOVE: *A yew arch takes some years to grow to its full height and maturity, as here. Drawing in ink on a photograph of your garden will give you an idea of what an arch like this would look like when fully grown.*

CREATING A FRAMEWORK

For different parts of a garden to combine into a satisfying whole, a cohesive structure is needed. Decide on your priority spaces and create the framework around them. Keep everything simple. Boundaries and divisions should have a unity that will provide a clear background for the planting and join up the spaces harmoniously. For example, walls should all use similar bricks, or all be rendered and painted the same colour. Hedging plants should be compatible – either all native shrubs or trees or one type of clipped evergreen. The lines of the framework, whether straight, curved or squared, should be clear and firm. This is one of the most important factors in garden design.

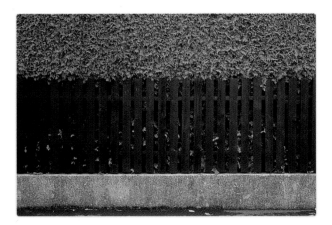

LEFT: Where garden meets roadside, this neat picket fence is backed by a rigorously clipped conifer hedge, both of which are very much in keeping with the feel of the garden as a whole.

❀ In gardens by the sea or on a hill, where strong winds and salt spray can damage all but the toughest of plants, the best sort of boundary is a hedge of mixed shrubs such as hawthorn, *Olearia*, escallonia, hazel and holly. This will act as a very effective shelter belt, within which more tender and colourful plants can be grown successfully.

THE PLANTED FRAMEWORK

IF YOU use only deciduous plants all the framework shape will be lost in winter when the leaves fall. Some deciduous plants have interesting trunks and branch shapes but you should include some kind of evergreen planting that will stand out clearly in winter.

Dividing the space into separate areas is a good way of preventing a long, narrow garden from looking like a ribbon, but the technique is also invaluable in many larger gardens to provide a variety of areas for different uses.

Boundary framework

❀ In small gardens, pyracantha and privet are often used as hedging plants along boundary walls. They provide good nesting sites for birds but they are greedy for space as well as water and nutrients, and in urban areas it is probably better to have trellis with climbers and evergreens, interspersed with the occasional evergreen shrub as a contrast and to break the straight line.

ABOVE: A clipped yew archway makes an attractive gateway to the front path and frames the view of a solid red brick house with its small portico.

❀ If the garden is bounded by a road, a clipped hedge often looks as neat as a wall and quite in keeping with the defined lines of the road. Beech makes a good and unusual hedge because, although it is not evergreen, it holds on to its leaves after they have turned colour and continues to provide protection and privacy throughout the winter.

Separating areas

❀ The framework for a formal garden is perhaps the easiest to design. You need a regular and level site. Once you have that, everything about the formal – its symmetry, regularity and mirror imagery – is in itself a framework. Low clipped hedges of box, taller clipped hedges of yew, clipped pairs of bay in tubs, a formal central fountain and paths crossing at right angles all reinforce the basic shape of the design. Everything adds

ABOVE: *There are many different ways to give a garden form. A trellis is a practical and attractive method of creating an enclosed area.*

ABOVE: *This narrow border of deep red roses and cotoneasters allows space for the pale old stone wall to be seen above the plants.*

up to a disciplined framework and, if it snows in winter, the whiteness emphasises the structure. An informal garden also needs its evergreens to create the framework, but the designer must be have an understanding of proportion and balance and trust his or her instincts.

❀ The most restful spaces are those with equal proportions, such as a circle or square. They make good seating areas or places in which to pause and relax. Long, narrow spaces, on the other hand, are an invitation to move on.

❀ Your framework should always define spaces that are there for a purpose. A circle should have entrances and exits. A path should lead somewhere; if it curves it should curve around something – a fountain, perhaps, or a feature shrub or sculpture. If it is dead straight, it should lead the eye to something intriguing.

THE BUILT FRAMEWORK

GARDEN structure consists of areas shaped by the vertical elements that surround and divide them. We have looked at ways in which planting can create divisions and surroundings. Now we can look at how built structures can reinforce and add to these areas.

❋ If you are dividing a playing area from a patio, you may want to be able to supervise what is going on in the sandpit or by the swing. You will therefore need to be able to see. Here you won't want a dense hedge, which would restrict your view, but you can create the effect of division by building a low wall or simply a pergola-type gateway. This will give the impression of entering a different area but you will still be able to supervise the children playing. Climbing roses or honeysuckle will soften the structure.

❋ An arch can be used to connect areas or to divide one area from another. It can be flanked on either side by a hedge or fence, but that is not always necessary. It will, all on its own, give the impression of a gateway into a different environment. There are many different types of arch. Tall, wide arches can be built at regular intervals, rather like a pergola but not so enclosed. If widely enough spaced, they will not cut out too much light and summer-flowering plants such as lavender can be grown beneath them so that you have a walkway to be enjoyed at leisure.

❋ The view through any arch should lead the eye to something interesting further down the garden – perhaps a sculpture, a gateway or a decorative shrub or urn.

❋ If you don't want to divide the garden with too many tall structures, low fences of trellis, provided the supporting uprights are sturdy and good looking, can provide elegant divisions while keeping an open vista at a higher level.

❋ Arbours and niches can divide up spaces, particularly if used on a corner where two paths intersect.

❋ Terraced gardens create good opportunities for structured framework. Long, shallow terraced gardens were popular in the 1920s and 30s. They had wide steps, balustrading and stone or brick cross paths and were often bounded by clipped box or yew on either side. The balustrading was often made of moulded concrete and it is very easy today to create a similar result with walls of concrete blocks, rendered and then painted. The walls should be no more than 45 cm (18 in) high so that people can sit on them.

Linking the compartments

❋ Having divided up the garden with a framework of planting or built structures, it is necessary to link the compartments or there will be no feeling of being one complete entity that a good garden needs. Use the same paving or brick for patios and paths throughout the garden. Walls should be topped with coping stones to match the paving, all of which will bring a sense of coordination and unity to the whole.

❋ When building pergolas, arbours and arches, again try to use similar materials that you have used throughout the whole garden. If you start off with a simple metal arch use the same metal for any more arches and for arbours. With their clean lines and simple shapes, these are particularly suitable for urban gardens. Similarly, if you start off with a wooden pergola, follow through with wooden furniture, wooden gates and so on.

ABOVE: *This unusual cherry-lined pergola has a double row of lavender at its feet, leading the eye to the gate and lake beyond.*

❀ A rustic pole screen can be used to divide a vegetable garden from the pleasure garden, but it should be in keeping with other divisions in the garden. Rough-cut wood would not be particularly suitable in conjunction with a sophisticated curved brick wall, for example, but would be perfectly acceptable if trellis or other wooden fences or evergreen hedges were used elsewhere.

The horizontal and the vertical

❀ When working out the structure, don't forget that you want a contrast between vertical and horizontal surfaces. Low hedges should be interrupted occasionally by a tall, conical tree or shrub. Expanses of open lawn should also have vertical interruptions here and there to keep the viewer interested.

RIGHT: *The multi-coloured brickwork on this terrace creates a pattern that is echoed by the careful planting.*

BELOW: *A rendered Italianate wall leads from a woodland garden through a rounded arch, giving an intriguing glimpse into the densely planted area beyond.*

INTEGRATING HOUSE AND GARDEN

The entrance to your garden is important. An interesting and inviting environment should greet you when you step out of the door. Not every door will open directly on to the garden, of course, but a row of well-tended pots could point the way to the garden, or perhaps a trellis-trained flowering climber on the wall. Remember that a level garden seen from the ground appears foreshortened and shorter than it really is. Individual compartments will seem shorter too; so if you are planning a circular lawn, the circle will seem squashed unless you make it more of an oval, with the longest part facing the house.

DOORWAYS AND WINDOWS

THE ideal entrance to a garden is through French doors to a patio. This really makes the garden into another 'room', and even when the weather is cool or rainy the garden 'picture' can be appreciated through the protective glass.

Single doors

❀ If a large entrance is not possible, the garden door can still be given glass panels, which will make it seem less remote from the house. A scented shrub next to the door and pots or containers of summer-flowering plants will also be welcoming. A pot of scented-leaved pelargoniums directly by the door will release their aroma as people brush against them. Lavender and rosemary will do the same.

Side entrance

❀ Some gardens can be reached only through a side entrance. Even if a side entrance is narrow and tunnel-like you can make it seem more spacious by painting the walls white.

ABOVE: An arched entrance leading from shadow into sunlight is one of the most romantic ways to approach an outdoor space. The wrought iron gates give the impression that you are entering a secret garden.

ABOVE: *These garden doors lead directly on to lush borders overflowing with flowers and fruit.*

❀ White reflects what light there is and always seems to enlarge a space. At the end of the alleyway you could install a wrought iron gate or arched entrance with climbers over it so that there is a hint of the promised garden before you get there. Always keep side entrances clear. There is nothing so off-putting as having to clamber over bags of compost or old prunings.

Windows

❀ Windows overlooking the garden should not be wasted but should look out on to a pleasant garden view. If the living-room window overlooks the garden, try to make sure the garden can be seen when people are sitting down.

❀ If this is not possible, you should at least ensure that some climbing plant or flowering tree is visible through the window. This is especially important for disabled or elderly people, who spend more of their time sitting down than others might.

Transitional entrances

❀ Porches, pergolas and conservatories all have very different functions but in one respect they are alike: they act as transitional areas between the house and the garden. Porches are usually erected as insulation from the weather. If they are very small they sometimes seem to act more as a barrier between house and garden than as a lobby joining one to the other. However, if they are glazed, they can be used to grow tender house-plants and become like miniature conservatories.

❀ A pergola by the garden door can complement the architecture of the house, while the planted elements can relate to the garden. A conservatory is also a meeting point between house and garden, relating both to the architecture and to the hardier plants outside.

ABOVE: *A narrow iron gate and enormous hydrangea entice you along the gravel path at the entrance to this garden.*

Proportion and scale

❀ Anything in the garden that is very large in relation to the house will seem excessive. Many a tree that is nicely in proportion when planted will grow far too large for its allotted space and not only prevent other things from growing but will diminish the house by its size. This is just as true of patios, terraces and paths.

❀ In a garden belonging to a small house, or a house with a narrow frontage, a grandiose patio will look out of place. A small patio with a carefully designed pattern of bricks or other paving and a concentration on the detailing and workmanship will look charming and could be surrounded by plants or a trellis, giving more of a courtyard effect.

❀ In a large house, on the other hand, elements that are too small will give a trivial, fussy effect. A broad terrace by the garden door will give the house a more

suitable visual base. Use large paving slabs, and have the terrace or patio running the length of the house, particularly if the house has large windows and patio doors. It should be wide enough to take a dining table and generously proportioned chairs.

❀ Courtyards offer good opportunities for brickwork or paving. Again, the materials and patterns should be in keeping with the house, and any flowerpots and containers should be of similar shape and colour.

The view towards the house

❀ Remember that when you are at the far end of the garden, you will get a different view of its relationship to the house that is just as important as the view from the house into the garden. The house becomes a focal point and you will be much more aware of materials that do not match or co-ordinate with those of the house and be pleasurably aware of those that do.

ABOVE: *The tall plants of* Romneya coulteri *here break the hard line of the window frame, creating a softer look.*

ABOVE: *On the street side of this house, a burgeoning* Ceanothus *softens the brickwork and anchors the house to the ground.*

Anchoring the house

❀ Planting evergreen shrubs near to the house helps to anchor it to the ground. This is especially true of new or modern houses, which can seem rather bleak and unrelated to their surroundings. Climbers are another excellent way of anchoring the house. Climbing plants that cover the whole house are good for buildings that have no particular architectural interest. Virginia creeper, which turns the most astonishingly bright red colour in autumn, does the job well.

❀ A traditional house with some architectural interest will be better with climbing roses around the windows and nothing else to hide the materials and design. Interesting modern buildings, some of which are sculptures in their own right, may not need anything clambering over them but could benefit from groups of bold architectural plants nearby to act as anchors.

Paths

❀ Paths leading directly from the house should be as wide as you can make them; narrow paths are less inviting. Two people should preferably be able to walk together in conversation. This is not always possible in small gardens but it is something to aim for. Paths can get narrower as they lead into the remoter parts of the garden, but near the house the path is acting as a gateway to the whole garden and should reflect that fact.

Security

❀ The way in which the garden relates to the house can influence security quite seriously. The street door should not be concealed by tall, dense shrubs, which would prevent a burglar being seen while trying to force the lock. Low planting is advisable here, which would make anyone trying to break in much more visible.

❀ At the back, avoid growing trees and shrubs near the house that a burglar could use as a ladder. If you want to clothe the house in greenery, stick to thorny plants such as the unfriendly climbing roses 'Mermaid' and 'Albertine', or a *berberis* or *pyracantha*.

❀ Make sure you have a place where you can lock up ladders and heavy garden implements such as spades and forks. Padlocking a ladder to the wall is better than leaving it lying about, and certainly never leave one propped up against a wall as an invitation to intruders.

ABOVE: *In the garden of this modern single-storey building, a wide gravel walkway takes you at a leisurely pace back to the house.*

ABOVE: *This small garden is made to seem much larger by the divisions and cross-axes. Here, a brick path leads to a blue seat as the focal point, with the view interrupted only by a large copper planter.*

GETTING TO WORK

Once you have thought carefully about how you want your garden to look, it's time to begin the hard work. Remember – every element of your house and garden must work together.

❀

You will want the garden to become a focal point, so think seriously about the position of your house and its relationship to the garden to get the maximum from it.

❀

Choose materials for your garden that will complement its style; use different types of paving to add shape and texture.

❀

Don't worry if you have a small or irregularly shaped plot. You can make its unusual aspects a design feature.

MAINTAINING LAWNS

A good lawn is an attractive feature but a poor one can
be a real eyesore. On clay soils in wet districts, for example, a really
green, healthy lawn is difficult to achieve. Many people tend to take
up unsatisfactory lawns and lay bricks or paving instead. However, if
you garden on clay and really would like to have an area of lawn, you
can lay new turfs on rafts of sand and rubble to ensure good drainage.
Lawns should be very slightly sloping to prevent waterlogging.
Aim for a minimum slope of 1 in 80 and a maximum slope of 1 in 4.
Steeper gradients are better terraced.

ABOVE: *A tiny tree in a lawn should not adversely affect the grass growth.
This maple makes a stunning contrast against a green backcloth of foliage.*

Grass for lawns

✿ There are different mixtures of grass for different
situations. For example, some will stand up to bikes
and ball games, some will grow satisfactorily in light
shade and some will produce the sort of velvety green
suitable for bowling greens but that is not so resilient
as the others.

Lawn shape

✿ Although a rectangle is probably the most common
shape for lawns, it is often more pleasing to have an
oval, circular or irregularly shaped lawn. Avoid small
and fussy curves and awkward corners, which are very
difficult to maintain and mow.

✿ If you want to include island beds, make sure the verges
are wide enough to take a mower. When deciding where
the lawn should go, remember that all parts of a lawn
need to receive some direct sunlight during the day so
try not to choose too shady a part of the garden.

Access to the lawn

✿ You should be able to reach the lawn from several
angles. If you approach the lawn along only one path
or one small entrance or gateway, the soil will become
compacted and the grass worn and brown. Paths
should run alongside the lawn rather than across it,
unless you choose to lay concrete stepping stones.

ABOVE: *Lawns do best under lightly canopied trees. This lawn is flourishing
under silver birches.*

* A path between a lawn and a flowerbed can be useful in wet weather, and summer flowers tumbling over a path do look attractive. Lay paths and stepping stones below the level of the lawn and leave a narrow grass-free mowing edge between the lawn and path to make mowing and edging easier.
* Avoid using loose chippings as a material for paths next to a lawn. They inevitably get kicked on to the grass and will damage the mower blades.

Lawns under trees

* Lawns will not thrive beneath a dense canopy of leaves. Shortage of light and water and the dripping water from the edges of the trees will make it difficult for the grass to grow properly. It will end up thin and wispy and moss will soon begin to encroach.
* Cutting the lower branches and shortening the higher ones may help a little but you are still never likely to achieve a good lawn. The best thing is to remove the turf completely from around the tree trunks and create a large bed for bulbs such as hardy cyclamen and crocuses and shade-loving plants such as periwinkles (*Vinca*) and dead nettles (*Lamium*).

ABOVE: *A well-situated lawn can be used as an outdoor room with judicious use of sunlight and shade and comfortable garden furniture.*

* Specimen trees can look marvellous when planted in a large expanse of green lawn. If you want to plant a tree in a small lawn, choose a small tree such as the cut-leaf Japanese maple (*Acer palmatum* 'Dissectum'), which will take 20 years to grow to 1.5 m (5 ft). *Acer japonicum* 'Aureum' will grow to 3 m (10 ft) and has attractive leaves, which provide colour from early spring to early autumn.

The non-grass lawn

* Although grass is certainly the most reliable material for a lawn, you can create small areas of lawn with other plants such as camomile or thyme. They do not have the resilience of grass and should not be walked on too much.
* A good place might be at the base of a fountain or in the centre of a circular herb bed. A popular plant for this kind of use is *Anthemis nobilis*.

PAVED AREAS, STEPS AND PATHS

Probably the first step in designing a garden is to incorporate a paved area for relaxation, entertainment and family meals. Paved areas near the house form important transitional meeting places between house and garden. Hard materials carry the architectural feel of the house out of doors. Planted containers and shrubs nearby bring in the garden element. Paths and steps also provide an architectural element and should be carefully planned, as they will become part of the basic framework. Stick to one or two basic materials throughout or the end result will be fussy.

ABOVE: *A small area outside the house has been attractively bricked in a square shape and surrounded by interesting and varied plants. Even the smallest outdoor space can be made into a pleasant spot.*

Patio shapes

❀ The shapes you use in all garden spaces will be among the important things that set the style of your garden. A symmetrical arrangement will give the space a formal look, whereas a curving, asymmetrical one will suit a more relaxed style and a geometric asymmetrical one will suit an abstract modern garden.

ABOVE: *You do not need very much space to create a small oval or circular seating area. This one is gravelled and has mostly green planting with a little seat for contemplation.*

❀ If your garden is surrounded by tall buildings, as is likely in an urban setting, straight, geometric lines generally work best, as they will complement the shapes of the surrounding buildings.

❀ In a small area it is best to stick to one shape, just as it is best to stick to very few materials. It is also best not to try and mix diagonals and curves or squares and circles. Even in larger gardens, there will be better unity and cohesion if you limit the number of different shapes.

❀ Once you have decided on the shapes for the paved areas, you can design the patterns for the bricks or paving you are going to use. There is all the difference in the world between well-laid paving in interesting patterns and concrete slabs carelessly placed on the ground.

❀ Paving patterns can be divided into those that are static and those that are dynamic. Static patterns hold the eye within the area and have a peaceful quality. Dynamic patterns lead the eye along a path or paved area with a feeling of movement, an invitation to explore further.

Types of paving

❀ There are numerous forms of paving to choose from. Pre-cast concrete is available in many forms, including slabs that vary in size, shape and thickness. Clay bricks in many colours and dark engineering bricks are suitable for many areas. Granite setts (paving blocks) and cobbles are ideal for small awkward areas.

❀ Concrete slabs interspersed with small areas of cobbles can break up the blandness of concrete on its own. Some paving materials become slippery when wet; others, like brick, are highly non-slip.

Combining gravel and paving

❀ If you have decided against lawns and soft surfaces in your garden, one paved area can lead to another through a series of enclosures and paths. The whole garden can be given an extended courtyard effect, which will provide plenty of space for sitting out and entertaining in the summer months.

❀ Some of the paving can be given over to gravel, with 'stepping stones' of paving slabs to give a firm foothold and plants growing in the gravel. Many plants like growing through gravel because it drains well but also helps to prevent moisture from evaporating too quickly.

❀ Many alpines and Mediterranean silver-leaved plants flourish and will seed themselves. There are various types of gravel to choose from, including white lime-stone, white gravel chippings and washed pea shingle, which has rounded edges. It is best not to use white gravel in sunny areas where the light shining on it can make it quite blinding.

ABOVE: *This circular paved area is surrounded by a shady pergola and furnished with folding chairs, which can easily be carried indoors in wet weather.*

DECKING AND OTHER USES FOR TIMBER

TIMBER decking is a natural material with simple lines, which can be practical and attractive in a number of different situations. It is often used as an alternative to paving. The combination of doors, flooring, fencing, furniture and steps all made of wood can help provide a unified look, which is simple yet stylish. Decking should ideally be made of hardwood, which needs no preservative treatment. Softwood must be planed or it will splinter, and it should be given preservative treatment, which should be repeated at regular intervals. Large areas of decking are not always successful in a cold, damp climate, where the timber may never have the chance to dry out fully and will eventually rot.

Construction

❀ An area of timber decking is not hard to construct. The decking timbers rest on beams and joists supported by posts held in the ground with concrete. This type of construction allows air to circulate, keeping the wood dry unless there are prolonged periods of snow or rain and the atmosphere remains moist.

Raised decking

❀ In the USA older houses were traditionally built with the living area above ground level, leaving space beneath for a cellar and to allow air to circulate. A wooden deck was often built as a way of extending the upper level to create an extra patio area.

❀ Decking is particularly suited to this form of extension because the air circulating around it helps to keep it dry and prevents the wood from rotting. However, it can also be used as a surfacing material at ground level. It is particularly suited to houses with timber clapboarding or shingled roofs and it can give a small space a pleasing look when used in conjunction with wooden fencing.

Decking on roof gardens

❀ Timber is a good material for roof gardens because it is much lighter in weight than other forms of paving. Many flat roofs have not been designed to carry heavy weights and decking will help to balance the weight of people walking on the roof.

❀ Square timber panels, similar in size to paving slabs, can be clamped together to provide flooring. They should be laid on a timber base above the roof finish so that water can drain to a downpipe. Before making any plans for a roof-garden you should find out whether you need permission to use it for this purpose and how much weight the roof can bear.

ABOVE: *Decking tiles in interesting patterns have been used here in geometric arrangements on two levels. Small blue glazed pots hold clipped evergreens that will be attractive all year.*

Decking and water

❁ Timber decking and water always look very natural together and landing stages for river boats have traditionally been made of decking. It can be useful for disguising the edges of artificial pools made with plastic liners and is also ideal for bridges.

❁ A real bridge can be constructed over a small pond or a mock bridge can be built to separate the pond from the water plants, thus making the pool seem bigger than it actually is. A 'landing stage' jutting out over a pond can be finished off with a timber balustrade, giving an attractive bird's eye view of the water. A small hump-backed timber bridge painted rich red is an excellent addition to a Japanese-style garden.

Timber decking in modern designs

❁ The regularly spaced lines created by boards of decking can be used to create exciting and attractive angles and changes of level. Timber decks look good in modern settings and make an excellent foil to plants and containers. Boards can also combine well with gravel, which on its own is not an ideal surface for wheelchairs or delicate shoes.

ABOVE: *This compact and well-stocked roof garden uses decking with rounded sea cobbles to soften it and add interest. A variety of evergreen, variegated and flowering shrubs provide interest all year.*

Wooden paths

❁ Wood is not often used for paths but might be a good choice as a continuation from a bridge or patio made of decking. Discs cut from tree trunks can be set into the ground but these usually look best in a fairly rural setting and are not suitable as a complement to decking used in sophisticated geometrical shapes. Discs are also likely to become slippery in wet weather so could be dangerous underfoot. Coarsely shredded bark can look attractive, although it looks better in a woodland or wild garden setting and is not right for a formal garden.

LEFT: *Decking and water combine well together. Here, decking is used along with brick to surround a pond with its lavish growth of evergreens and windmill-like sails, purposely designed to give shade.*

DEALING WITH AWKWARDLY SHAPED GARDENS

❦

Many gardens are awkwardly shaped. They may be very narrow
or have been squashed in between buildings on a new estate.
They may narrow at one end to create a triangular plot.
Basement gardens often have tiny patio spaces with very steep
steps leading to dry gardens overshadowed by neglected trees.
All these problems may be seen as challenges rather than
disadvantages. There are many ways of approaching the solutions.

LONG NARROW GARDENS

GARDENS belonging to terraced houses are often long
and narrow, sometimes almost ribbon-like in shape.
The danger with this sort of garden is that it can feel
more like a passageway than a garden. The part nearest
the house may get used as a sitting-out area, but the rest
of the garden is a repository for old furniture, and stinging
or prickly weeds. One of the following solutions may suit
this sort of garden.

A series of rooms

❀ The most obvious and usually most successful
answer is to divide the plot into a series of separate
compartments linked by a path. Each compartment
can then be filled with a symmetrical design based on
a square, a circle or an oval. By dividing the plot in
this way you may be able to use the dividing barriers
to hide an ugly barbecue or an intrusive large shrub or
tree or to disguise a shed or screen a distant telegraph
pole seen over the garden fence.

❀ The different areas will allow you to do much more
with the garden. You might combine a small shrubbery
or woodland area in which you could conceal a small
shed, with a special play area with a swing and sandpit
or a formal water garden with a fountain. If your main
interest is in plants and growing things, one of these
areas could be a small vegetable plot or could be
devoted to growing show flowers.

Geometric divisions

❀ Rather than separating the areas with hedges or
shrubs, you could use low walls and paving shapes to
create interest and variety. Use diagonal lines, which
will help to make the garden seem wider. A diagonal
brick-lined pool could face a diagonal brick patio
outside the garden door.

❀ A path could lead to the next area, perhaps a small
lawn with flower-beds around it. The path could then
lead on to a small barbecue area. To prevent this sort

ABOVE: A raised wooden walkway built about a pond and bog garden allow
the visitor to gaze down on to the water and the spectacular collection of irises.

of layout from seeming too flat, you could add vertical elements at strategic points. These might be small trees or carefully placed shrubs, arches or small pergolas.

❀ Each compartment should invite the visitor in with a visual surprise such as a sculpture, a water feature or an architectural plant and should have some form of seat so that people can stay and enjoy it.

A garden walk

❀ For extra narrow gardens, an alternative to the idea of separate garden spaces is to devote the whole garden to a deliberate garden walk. This will make the most of its narrowness. A path leading in gentle curves down the centre of the plot will create undulating borders on either side.

❀ Recesses or arbours can be created at intervals, where people can sit and read or relax and savour the flowers and their scents. At the end there should be a reward for those who have made the journey – a still pool, perhaps, or a fountain or statue. This kind of garden offers opportunities for urns and statuary at intervals along the walk and plenty of opportunities for formal or romantic planting.

ABOVE: Long, narrow gardens can be made to look more spacious by the addition of features such as walkways or recesses and arbours. Perhaps you could place a fountain or a statue at the end.

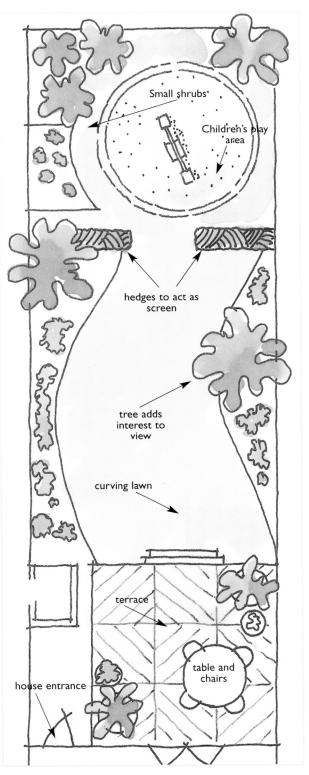

Small shrubs

Children's play area

hedges to act as screen

tree adds interest to view

curving lawn

terrace

table and chairs

house entrance

ABOVE: This garden is long and narrow, like many town gardens. The borders contain plants of varying heights to conceal the edges, and the whole garden has been divided into 'rooms', each with its own character. The patio is near the house, separated from the compost heap by a hedge. The lawn is slightly curved to give a feeling of movement, and the children's play area occupies the end of the garden.

SMALL FRONT GARDENS

GENERALLY, urban front gardens are difficult to cope with because they are often quite heavily shaded and also have to hold the rubbish bins. It is easy to give up on them completely but thoughtful planning can transform a front garden into a really attractive welcoming feature to the house.

❀ The first thing is to create some structure for the rubbish bin, where it will be easily accessible but concealed from people going in and out of the front door. Something simple, such as a three-sided 1-m (3-ft) tall brick enclosure is a good answer. One open side means the bin can be easily removed for empty-ing. A carefully constructed shed is less useful, being difficult both to keep clean and to maintain.

❀ Front gardens are seldom used for sitting in, being too public, but they do mark the approach to your home and should be well designed and welcoming. It is best to create a garden that will not require too much maintenance. Front gardens are often the forgotten areas of the gardener's domain and receive little watering, feeding or weeding.

❀ An important rule for the tiny garden is not to try to squeeze too many plants into it and it is often best to go for formality. Eliminate all grass, lay paving and install pairs of large pots planted with clipped bay or

ABOVE: *This house sits directly on the pavement but its owners have managed to 'green' the area with planted boxes of ivy and colourful hanging baskets.*

box. A small weeping tree in the centre of the plot can create an attractive feature. The weeping pear (*Pyrus salicifolia* 'Pendula') makes an excellent specimen tree in a small space and has a charming arching habit and pretty silvery leaves.

❀ Alternatively, go for a more informal look. This is not always easy in a small space and it is tempting to put in too many plants, which will soon grow out of control.

❀ One answer is to cover the whole area with gravel or pebbles and create a Japanese garden with a rock or two placed at judicious intervals and a silver-leaved plant to balance them. Otherwise, colourful groupings of pelargoniums or busy Lizzies (*Impatiens*) can brighten up a front garden magically. All these ideas will draw the eye away from the walled-off area of the rubbish bin and create a positive impression on those walking by.

ABOVE: *Front gardens should be simple and welcoming. This one has matching blue paint on the front door and planting boxes, which looks spectacular against the white walls. The two miniature willows with their attractive variegated foliage create a light, optimistic mood.*

ABOVE: *This restrained but effective planting scheme with one ivy-covered wall and a ribbon of pink in front of a cotoneaster hedge suits this modern house.*

SLOPING SITES

IF YOUR garden is on a slope, you can create a wild meadow or sloping lawn, but other choices are limited because water will drain away quickly and many plants will suffer. In general it is better to terrace the site, using low walls to contain the different levels.

- ❀ For retaining walls use materials that complement the house itself. Brick houses look better with their garden walls and paths made of similar coloured bricks.
- ❀ For stone houses, try to use stone for retaining walls and paths. Rendered or pebble dash houses look best with concrete walls, rendered and then painted. Modern outdoor paints are available in a wide range of excellent colours. All walls should be topped with coping stones, which overlap the wall by about 4 cm (1½ in). Steps should be as wide and as shallow as the space will allow, using similar materials to the walls and paths.
- ❀ Each level of terracing can be treated differently. One level could be planted with yellow and orange plants, for example, while further down oranges, reds and purples could take their place; further down again, misty blues and mauves would seem to disappear gently into the distance.
- ❀ If the site is shady, this colour transition will not work so well, because you will not be able to grow the variety of plants necessary. Here a formal terrace could lead down to a less formal collection of mixed shrubs and herbaceous plants or a quiet seating area with a pool or fountain.

BASEMENT GARDENS

BASEMENT gardens often consist of a very narrow patio with steep, narrow steps leading up to the garden, which is normally too high to be viewed from below. The patio itself can feel cramped and dark and is not an inviting place to sit. In such cases, it may be best to sacrifice some of the growing space by making the patio a little larger and the steps a little more generous, giving you the opportunity to make both patio and garden more attractive.

ABOVE: *Steps should be as wide and shallow as space allows when leading from one area of terracing to another.*

WATER AND LIGHTING

Water has a magical quality in a garden. Quite literally, of course,
it brings life to the garden, since nothing will grow without it.
Added to that, the sight and sound of water bring liveliness,
light and movement unmatched by anything else. Combined
with effective lighting, you can transform your garden into a brilliant
and enchanted place. Both water and lighting offer the opportunity
for beautiful and unexpected features.

ABOVE: *A long, narrow garden deceives the eye with the creation of a pond
and a wooden bridge with a bright red hand rail, followed by a paved seating
area beyond. The edges are concealed by evergreen planting.*

STILL WATER

PONDS and pools offer tranquillity. In the open they can
reflect the sky with a delightful magical mirror effect
of light. Such smooth planes of water can act as a foil to
planting either in the water or next to it. A pool should
be treated as an integral part of the garden's plan and
should be built of materials sympathetic to the shape, size
and materials of the garden and house. You can choose
to have a natural-looking pool in an organic shape or you
can give it a much more formal aspect with hard stone or
tiles and a symmetrical shape.

Formal pools

✿ Formal pools look at home in symmetrical gardens,
set in paving or some other hard surface and reached
by straight paths or set in a terrace or courtyard. They
can be sunken or raised and will reflect the stone or
brick as well as any water lilies grown in them. They
make excellent homes for ornamental fish, which can
be observed at close quarters.
✿ Geometric shapes work best for formal pools – it is
hard to beat a rectangular pond. A short wide one

PLANTS FOR POOLS

WATER lilies (*Nymphaea*) are the ideal plants to
grow in a formal pool. They like the stillness
of the water and their flowers seem to float upon it.
Hardy water lilies include *Nymphaea* 'Escarboucle',
which is vigorous with large red blooms; *N.* 'Helvola'
has dainty, star-shaped canary yellow flowers throughout summer and is good for a tub or small pool;
N. 'Hermine' has white flowers over a long period.

will look good on a terrace, whereas a long narrow one, more like a canal, will look good beside a straight path or as the centrepiece in a narrow garden. Small circular, sunken ponds can look very pretty in tiny gardens. Ideally, this sort of pond should form an important feature in the garden and not be tucked away out of sight.

Wildlife pond

❀ You do not need a very large pond to attract wildlife and grow moisture-loving plants. A pond 1 m (3 ft) across is quite big enough to have its own population of water insects, damsel flies, frogs and toads. If you place your pond near a flower border, the plants will provide cover for shy creatures to hide in. A lawn nearby will provide an open space for birds. If the pond is completely surrounded by lawn or paving, remove some of the turf or slabs so that you can create a bog or rock garden or a wild flower patch, which will give shelter to small creatures. If young children are going to be playing in the garden you may want to avoid open water but you can still create a small boggy area for wildlife by digging a hole, lining it as for a pond, but filling it with soil.

BOG PLANTS

Marginal plants for the shallow edges include the yellow flag iris (*Iris pseudacorus*), marsh marigolds (*Caltha palustris*) and *Veronica beccabunga*. Leaves that float on the surface provide shade for underwater creatures and help prevent algae. They include water soldiers (*Stratiotes aloides*) and fringed water lilies (*Nymphoides peltata*). Plants for permanently wet soil near the pond include bugle (*Ajuga reptans*), creeping Jenny (*Lysimachia nummularia*) and lady's smock (*Cardamine pratensis*).

ABOVE: *Ponds respond wonderfully well to planting, reflecting tall, elegant plants particularly well in the water. It is always best to keep the planting simple. Here, yellow water irises and water lilies make a spectacular show.*

ABOVE: *Still water gives interesting and beautiful reflections as well as visions of the bottom of a pool. In shallow water, small water-loving plants will grow well around cobbles and over stones.*

MOVING WATER

ADDING movement to water creates a truly magical effect. Reflections are enhanced, the sound of moving water is soothing and musical, and fish benefit from the enhanced oxygenation of the water. Water lilies, however, prefer still water, so are better suited to ponds without fountains, or where a fountain is offset so that part of the pond remains still. Movement can be created by fountains, waterspouts, rills or cascades and is guaranteed to bring sparkle and dash to the garden. As always, it should be planned in scale with the area. A gentle trickle can be refreshing in a small garden, where a large fountain would be pretentious.

ABOVE: *An elegant formal fountain with a tall jet surrounded by smaller ones. The pale adjacent pink brick paving includes beds of lavender.*

ABOVE: *This sculpted glass fountain alters subtly as you walk around it, catching the sun and glittering as the water runs down it.*

Cascades

❀ Cascades have frequently been used in great and grand gardens, especially in Italy, to create spectacular stairs of water. The splendid cascade at Chatsworth in Derbyshire was built in 1694 and still amazes visitors with its tumbling staircase of water. It is quite possible to make more modest cascades in keeping with smaller gardens.

❀ On a sloping site, a narrow channel, interrupted at intervals by a short cascade and an occasional octagonal or round pool, can create an enchanted atmosphere like that of a Persian or Moorish garden.

❀ On a flat site, an informal cascade can be built quite easily, the water being circulated by a small electric pump.

❀ An unusual cascade suitable for a small informal garden can comprise a series of watering cans or urns lying on their sides, each emptying into the one below to create a kind of cascade. This idea could be developed in different ways using a variety of receptacles.

Fountains

❀ Fountains have become popular recently, partly because of the availability of comparatively inexpensive reproductions of traditional designs, and partly because of the mass production of small submersible pumps, supplied with a fountain rose jet and sold in kit form. Installed in a part of the garden that becomes very hot during the day, a fountain has a distinctly cooling effect.

❀ Reproductions and copies of traditional fountain designs such as dolphins and cherubs are widely available. There are also some modern metal fountains in the form of leaves, twigs or birds, in which the water cascades down from one section to another.

OTHER TYPES OF WATER FEATURE

THERE are any number of ways of getting a small amount of water to bubble, trickle, flow or glint in a decorative and refreshing way. You can introduce the sound of running water by running it through a pipe in the wall, using one of the cheapest electric pumps and a small cistern.

Cobbles

❀ Rounded pebbles collected together are popular as a base for water to trickle over. (These are widely available from garden centres so please do not collect them from beaches.) A cobble fountain is simple and pleasant and does not need a pool. The effect relies on the sound and movement of water splashing over the stones into a reservoir; the water is constantly recycled.

❀ You will need a tank large enough for a submersible pump and holding enough water to cope with evaporation from the surface of the cobbles on a sunny day. The size of the reservoir will depend on how often the system is topped up – it need be no bigger than a plastic bucket.

Millstones

❀ A large millstone can have a striking architectural impact so should be carefully placed where it will balance

some other strong feature. The water falls over the side of the stone and is collected in a reservoir below; again, no pool is required. A geyser jet can be used to introduce air if you want a more turbulent effect.

Bamboo spout

❀ In Japanese gardens, bamboo canes are used as spouts. Balanced on an upright, the cane fills up with water, tips it out on to pebbles below, then starts all over again. Some people find the regular filling and emptying peaceful, others find it monotonous.

BELOW: *A traditional Japanese bamboo spout deposits water into a large stone bowl that stands on a craggy rock with cobblestones below.*

LIGHTING SYSTEMS

ELECTRICITY in the garden has made it possible to create effective lighting schemes from the smallest to the largest gardens, and has equally made it possible to water the garden effectively and economically over a long period, even when you are not there. For garden lighting always use lights specifically designed for outdoor use. Any other lighting is dangerous if used outside.

Advantages of garden lighting

✿ Lighting adds another dimension to the garden and should be planned into your scheme from the beginning. A well-designed scheme can turn your garden into a completely different world at night. You can create subtle pools of light with a general illuminating effect or dramatically highlight particular trees, shrubs and garden features.

✿ The eye is intrigued and delighted by small lights nestling among the foliage and flowers of large containers and plants in surrounding beds. It is usually more flattering to light the garden rather than the house, unless your house has unusual or striking architectural features that merit special highlighting.

How much light?

✿ For typical suburban gardens, one or two small flood-light fittings mounted on the back wall of the house will provide enough light for moving about safely and enable a patio area to be used for barbecues. However, much more can be done to highlight aspects of the garden plan or planting and make the garden more fascinating at night.

✿ Focal points such as sculptures and fountains can look particularly effective when well lit. Remember, though, even when aiming for dramatic effects, subtlety is important. It is very easy to be over-enthusiastic and overdo the lighting, ending up with something glaring and uncomfortable.

BELOW: *A handmade ceramic Japanese lamp gives the garden a pleasant glow in the dark and will guide you along a path.*

Lighting the outdoor room

❀ Lighting is particularly important where the garden is small and designed to be used for entertaining in the evening, as well as for displaying the plants. Here you want not only to highlight plants seen from the sitting area, which may be at the far end of the garden, but also to light the path leading to it. This lighting does not need to be as bright as daylight but bright enough to see where you are going, yet leaving the rest of the garden mysterious.

❀ A collection of small candle-lit lamps can light up a table perfectly adequately, casting a becoming light on both objects and people. There are many different and attractive glass and perforated metal holders for candles and nightlights and the flickering of a live flame creates interesting moving shadows.

Lighting seen from the house

❀ If you don't go into the garden at night, but want to be able to admire it from indoors or from the patio, you do not need to light the paths and can concentrate mainly on the 'picture' from the windows.

❀ Highlight decorative foliage, sculptures and other features. You will probably find that individual branches you have not really noticed before will respond like magic to being lit at night and will become positively sculptural when individually highlighted.

ABOVE: *Unobtrusive light sources are by far the most effective for night lighting. Here, the light source is hidden by the trees, giving a dramatic effect.*

Positioning garden lights

❀ A little lighting, if well positioned, can have a tremendous impact. Avoid dazzle and glare by keeping fittings and bulbs hidden. There are all sorts of places where you can do this, such as behind tree trunks or walls, or behind plant containers or large-leaved shrubs. Try out their positions by placing lights temporarily and then walk around the garden to check that the light source is properly concealed from all angles.

❀ Spike lamps are useful because they can be moved around but they should be regarded as temporary only and not for permanent installation. The plug should be removed from its socket and the lamp taken into the house when not being used. As with all lamps, it is important to use the bulb recommended by the manufacturer or there may not be a watertight seal and the lamp might shatter.

Lighting trees

❀ The texture and shape of tree trunks, branches, leaves and blossom provide endless opportunities for decorative lighting. Use tungsten halogen flood spotlights, positioned to shine upwards into the branches from a garden wall or on to a lower part of the tree trunk.

❀ You can fix a light fitting at the centre of the tree to create a soft glow. Strings of fairy lights strung through the branches give a magical effect, particularly if the bulbs are all white. Make sure you use lights designed for outdoor use.

❀ Bulb holders on this sort of lighting should be moulded on to the cable; the type with sharp contacts that bite through the insulation of the cable to make connection with the cores are extremely dangerous if they are used outside.

The magic of light and water

❀ Water and light are a magical combination and at night can provide extra glitter and sparkle. Use wide and narrow beam spotlights on fountains and moving water. When lighting a pond make sure that the source of the light is not reflected in it, which would diminish the mystery.

Lighting for safety

❀ You should always have some lights to show steps and other changes of level and check that these do not cast confusing shadows. There should also be enough lighting near the house so that when you come out of the bright light of the house interior or the patio, you are not blinded by the sudden darkness.

Light fittings

❀ As with all other elements of the garden's design, the light fittings themselves should be in keeping with the garden's style. There are many good-looking functional fittings available, made of high-grade materials to resist corrosion and sealed against the weather. They are therefore not cheap.

❀ Several designs will hold energy-efficient, compact fluorescent bulbs and any fitting designed to use standard light bulbs could take one of these. Several low-level light sources are more pleasing than a few very bright ones but it does mean that the cost can very quickly mount up.

BELOW: *Lighting on water can produce a magical effect; here the different colours of the the lights give added interest.*

ABOVE: *Fairy lights twisted around the arches of this walkway enhance the flowers.*

❀ Light fittings powered by the sun are available. They can make good guiding lights, but the range of fittings available is not very large and some of them look as though they were designed for hotels rather than domestic gardens.

Installation

❀ All outdoor lighting should be installed by an approved specialist electrical contractor. Connections must be properly sealed and wiring must be of a special type, set in a conduit. Outdoor lighting is not cheap so test your chosen lights and make sure they are in the right places before you call in the contractor. Remember that plants will grow and the garden will change. Permanent lights that are very complicated to install should therefore be positioned beneath mature trees and shrubs or sculptural items that are unlikely to change position.

CONSTRUCTING
OUTBUILDINGS

Small buildings in the garden contribute greatly to efficiency and
often to the garden's charm as well. On the practical side, they
provide shelter and essential storage space for garden equipment and
furniture. They make pleasant places for conversation, shelter and
refreshment and can be excellent play spaces for children. Visually
they can contribute in an important way to the look of the garden,
providing architectural balance to the house or to some other structure
in the garden. Buildings of all kinds are potential focal points, used
to draw the attention and provide interest and entertainment. They
can also be eyesores, of course.

THE BASIC SHED

REASONABLY priced sheds are available in kit form to put
together at home. The smallest are large enough to
hold garden tools, folding furniture and games equipment.
The most basic garden sheds are not particularly pretty, but
there are ways in which they can be hidden. It is surprising
how often sheds are placed against a wall in the middle of
a small garden, where you cannot avoid looking at them.

BELOW: *Garden sheds are available to buy in kit form; they can be as basic
or sophisticated as your budget dictates.*

❀ If the garden is not quite rectangular and has the odd
awkward corner, this might be the very place to put a
small shed. Tuck it away out of sight behind some sort
of screen, perhaps a shrubbery or trellis with attractive
climbers trained over it.

❀ Try to focus attention on some other interesting feature
and away from the shed itself. It should be reached by a
path so that it is easy to get to, even in wet weather.

❀ There are many different sizes of shed available and
the more robust ones can be converted into work-
rooms with extra windows put in. They do not make
particularly attractive buildings from the outside but
should not be difficult to camouflage with paint or
conceal with shrubs and climbing plants.

Alternatives for small gardens

❀ If your garden is very small and there is no room for a
full-height shed, you can get seats-cum-storage units,
large enough to hold implements such as spades, forks
and trowels, small enough to place on the patio and
attractive enough to hold their own with the regular
patio furniture.

Brightening up a shed

❀ There have been great steps forward in exterior paints
in the last few years. You can paint almost anything
now in paint that will withstand the weather and
comes in an exciting range of colours, from wonderful
sea greens and blues to old rose and sunflower yellow.

❀ With these paints you can customise your shed by painting it in pale blue and white stripes, like a beach hut, for example, or in a really deep blue or green, perhaps outlining door and window frames in a different lighter colour.

Garden rooms

❀ As homes become smaller and more people work from home, creating an extra room in the garden to use as a studio or office makes a lot of sense. There are many companies who specialise in building such rooms, so you can get an attractive chalet-type building or a cottage-like 'second home'.

❀ Shop around for different designs and qualities – prices vary enormously. One thing you must be sure of is that it will be weathertight and warm. You can quite easily carry electricity via special cables buried underground so that you can run lighting, heating and computer equipment in the room. You need to make sure that doors and windows can be safely secured and that the room is properly insulated.

ABOVE: *This very basic garden shed has acquired a personality all of its own by being painted a bright sea-blue. This colour seems to show up the foliage particularly well.*

BELOW: *A well-ordered garden shed is a tremendous asset in any garden, however small. It is the perfect place to keep packets and tins, seeds and seed trays and other garden paraphernalia.*

CONVERSATORIES

THE purpose of buildings that use glass is to make full use of the sun and the daylight. The conservatory is a useful, weatherproof link between inside and outside, but it can also create a magic of its own. In this extension of the home you can enjoy the jungle atmosphere of tender plants with their bright colours and exotic scents. You can use it as a light and airy dining room or a quiet space in which to read or snooze. Cane or perforated metal chairs and tables will emphasise the tropical aspect, and plenty of tropical plants and climbers in containers will add to the 'holiday' feeling.

Conservatory style

❋ Most conservatories are attached to the house and great care should be taken to choose one whose style, proportions and materials are in keeping with the materials and the architecture of the house. This does not necessarily mean that all buildings should be of the same period. In fact, a simple modern construction added to a traditional house can look very much in keeping. Getting the scale and proportion right in relation to the house are by far the most important things, especially as conservatories are not cheap.

❋ Many conservatories are made of treated softwood and will require frequent painting, which is tricky and time-consuming. Cedar can be used unpainted and will weather to an attractive silver grey. Aluminium is expensive but almost maintenance free, as is UPVC.

❋ Georgian houses suit simple conservatories with arched windows and square panes, rather like the original orangeries popular in the 18th century for growing citrus fruits brought back from the Mediterranean. Victorian buildings, which are usually more eccentric and decorative, look good with a more flamboyant conservatory, perhaps with an ornamental metal frame, pointed windows and other Gothic detailing.

❋ Small cottages and houses suit small conservatories, which bridge the transition between house and garden without being too dominating.

ABOVE: *This Gothic-style greenhouse/conservatory is firmly based on brick foundations. It blends in well with the garden, while the planting around it also helps to make it 'fit in'.*

RIGHT: *A wrought-iron pavilion is a good focal point with its white painted curlicues and decorative seat. The whole effect is enhanced by an evergreen backdrop and a froth of Alchemilla mollis.*

Simple designs with aluminium or UPVC frames and no frills will often look better than anything which is more sophisticated.

❀ It is easy to be tempted by the advertisements for 'period' conservatories. Many are over-ornamented, however, with decorative details that are completely wrong for the house. With conservatories, as with so much in the garden, simplicity is usually more effective than too much detailing.

A focal point

❀ A good-looking greenhouse can be a focal point in a small garden. The hexagon is an attractive shape, and hexagonal greenhouses with wood or aluminium frames can look charming. It can be used as a display area for colourful plants such as pelargoniums, busy Lizzies (*Impatiens*) and tender fuchsias, for example, as well as for growing seeds and cuttings.

Pavilions and gazebos

❀ Pavilions are largely built for romantic atmosphere in larger gardens and to give a sheltered resting place with a view on to the garden. The idea comes from ancient Rome, from ancient Chinese pagodas and Indian Mogul temples or pavilions. A gazebo is a smaller version of a pavilion.

❀ Pavilions are often circular or hexagonal, giving a view on to the garden from all sides. The roof should have a high pitch to give it a more commanding presence and elegance. Wreathed in foliage, it will offer an agreeable contrast between the geometry of the materials and the free form of the planting.

❀ A Chinese pavilion looks marvellous with light bulbs picking out the exaggerated shape of the roof at night. Pavilions and gazebos should be positioned in a sunny part of the garden but with some planting to ensure a certain amount of shade and seclusion.

BELOW: *This Victorian conservatory is very tall and is able to hold quite large trees.*

USING GARDEN ORNAMENTS

Sculpture, in its most simple form, is placed in gardens to
provide pleasing shapes or as a way of marking and emphasising
spaces and contrasts, as a focal point or surprise, and to give a sense
of movement or stillness. Traditionally, sculpture had a certain symbolism
but, in general, this is not so meaningful today. Sculptures are used to
create a dramatic effect or as an eye-catcher at the bottom of a long vista.
The reason they work so well is that sculptures and other ornamental
objects stand in complete contrast to the forms and colours of plants. Even
'found' sculptures, such as granite boulders, and 'collected' sculptures of
piles of pebbles can act as a contrast to the flexible and soft forms
of things growing in the garden.

ABOVE: *Bright ornamental glass balls provide a dash of colour in
a snowy landscape.*

What sculpture?

❀ Many people associate sculpture with traditional
western forms such as large stone or lead figures from
Classical literature. These are too large, too grand and
too steeped in the past to look at home in many of
today's small gardens.

❀ However, sculpture incorporates many other objects
that can add interest, focal points, humour or romance
to a garden. During the 20th century sculptors have
explored abstract forms and different ways of depicting
figures, and many of these are eminently suited to the
modern garden.

ABOVE: *These eyecatching stone frogs appear to be sheltering underneath a
hanging stone.*

LEFT: *Sculptures do not need to take pride of place. Some are most effective if 'chanced upon', such as this modern head of a young boy peeping out from behind a curtain of ivy.*

❀ A figurative sculpture can look spectacular in an alcove or bower. In general, one piece or a pair should dominate. Too many sculptures will compete with each other for attention and lose their individual impact.

Choosing sculptures

❀ Always use sculptures with discretion. If they are too fussy they will compete with the plants for attention. If they are too big, they will compete with the view. They may be in stark contrast with their surroundings or cunningly hidden among greenery.

❀ Traditional figures of shepherds and shepherdesses, and cherubs and nymphs should be smaller than their classical counterparts for most gardens today. There are many concrete-based copies available, which can look enchanting placed under a tree or hidden in a rose arbour. Modern sculpture is often abstract, lending itself to modern gardens and acting as a marvellous foil to foliage.

Uses of sculpture

❀ A sculpture may be large or small, temporary or permanent, prominent or half-hidden. Whatever its qualities, it should reflect the tastes of its owner and the style and size of the garden. A sculpture can attract attention to the end of an alley or become an integral part of a group of shrubs or trees.

❀ A figure or urn can be used to emphasise a particular aspect of the garden, such as an inviting green path or a pool or enclosed courtyard, or to draw the eye so that visitors are led around the garden to discover what will be around the next corner.

Placing sculptures

❀ Sculptures should be deliberately placed to create an impact. You can commission a piece specially for a particular place in the garden, or choose a piece you like and then find a place for it. You could search for objects such as brightly coloured glass fishing floats, which look sculptural, and hang them from trees or place them on stones or pedestals.

❀ Sculptures should always be positioned in strategic places – at the end of a vista, grouped in an open grove or balanced by a group of shrubs or other strong planting. A strong piece can be used as a distant eye-catcher to be seen from a rise in the ground. Pairs of urns are effective at the top of steps or as a gateway to a different area of the garden.

ABOVE: *The globe is an appealing shape. This glass globe has the added fascination of water that flows over its surface, altering the flowers seen through it.*

URNS AND VASES

THESE are important as garden ornaments. Like figurative sculpture, a large urn may be used as a focal point at the end of an avenue or vista, or as a terminal feature on a gatepost. Identical urns or vases on pedestals may be used in rows to line a path, with a backdrop of clipped yew to draw attention to their shape. Sometimes they may be planted with some eye-catching plant such as a single palm or a collection of silver and pink bedding plants. Sometimes they look best standing on their own.

❀ Antique urns and vases are very expensive but there are good reproductions in various materials that can give the right impression. Simple terracotta pots are available in many sizes, are comparatively cheap and can look very impressive. Reproduction troughs are also available in cement-based artificial stone and can look imposing on a terrace.

ORNAMENTAL FURNITURE

SEATS and tables take up a fairly large space in the garden. Too often they spoil the effect by being of unsympathetic materials or simply too large for their environment. Putting a group of furniture on a special area of paving helps give it a purposeful look and acts as a framework. Scale is important. It may be a good idea to enclose the area partially so that the furniture's bulk does not intrude visually into the garden.

❀ Plastic furniture, although cheap, lightweight and easy to move about, cannot be said to add aesthetically to a garden. It may be the most convenient sort of furniture to have on a patio, but for permanent seats and benches, which become part of the garden design, there are more sympathetic materials to choose from.
❀ One seat placed in a niche, or angled against a group of shrubs or tall perennials, can look very sculptural. Stone seats are undeniably sculptural, although they are best positioned where they will warm up in the sun before you sit on them. Wrought iron can look graceful; treated, painted or stained timber looks particularly good in the context of a country-style garden. A bench can be 'settled' into its place with plants at the sides. This makes furniture look as though it has rooted and gives it a permanent look.
❀ A tree seat can run fully or half-way around a tree, providing a shady place in which to relax and an eye-catching decoration. Cast-iron reproduction

Victorian furniture looks particularly good in rather overgrown, informal gardens. Attractive cast-aluminium copies have the advantage of being light, but they do tend to lose the detailing of the decoration.

RIGHT: *Terracotta has great possibilities in the garden. This unusual and elegant tall pot is used to add architectural value to a patio.*

BELOW: *A traditional decorated terracotta urn can look good in a formal or informal setting. In a formal setting urns are best used in pairs or rows. Here, the background is somewhat overgrown and informal.*

PLANT CONTAINERS

WELL-grouped plant containers add a touch of luxury to a small courtyard, a porch or front door or the edge of a pool. The plants themselves contribute to the sculptural look so must be chosen carefully to enhance and complement the container. A large container with a short pelargonium poking out of the top will not look sculptural, no matter how colourful the plant.

❧ A timber half-barrel will hold a fairly large shrub and would look good with a standard clipped bay tree, particularly in country settings. A sophisticated alternative is the Versailles tub, which looks splendid planted with a lemon tree. Stone or tufa troughs can be planted with alpines or annuals.

❧ Metal buckets are unusual but attractive containers and look surprisingly good positioned on decking. Tall terracotta 'Ali Baba' urns with narrow necks are graceful and imposing on their own and best left unplanted.

BELOW: *This stone pedestal carries an elaborate container of helichrysum; a little stone pig sits to one side.*

Placing pots

❧ When using pots in groups try to keep similar materials and shapes together, otherwise there will be a lack of unity and the group will look fussy. Unglazed terracotta pots look good with each other but not so good with colour-glazed pots from China, for example. Stone pots look best sitting on stone paving and terracotta is best on brick, while stainless steel or galvanised metal buckets are popular for modern gardens and give a bright, fresh look to roof gardens. A pair of pots placed on either side of a front door may be planted with well-cared-for topiary yew, bay or box and will imply a welcome to visitors. Square pots are a good choice for the entrance to a rectangular area of garden, confirming its shape.

BELOW: *A tall, elegant, squared pot in the brightest indigo makes a striking focal point and co-ordinates with the rather paler grey-blue trellis behind it.*

GARDEN STYLES

There are two ways of approaching the design of a garden – the planned and the informal. Most garden styles fit into one of these.

Planned gardens are based on a central axis with cross-axes running at right angles dividing the garden into compartments. Informal gardens are curvaceous and natural looking.

✿

Within these two styles there are many different possibilities. Romantic, wildlife and exotic gardens tend to be informal, while roof gardens or tiny front gardens lend themselves to careful planning.

✿

Decide which effect you want to achieve before you start work on your garden and remember that it is not usually a good idea to combine planned and informal styles.

INFORMAL GARDENS

❦

Informal gardens are characterised by flowing curves, non-symmetrical arrangements of features and spaces, and plants that are allowed to grow into their natural shapes. Traditionally, gardens have always had their most formal areas near the house, gradually becoming more informal as they get further away. This still makes sense today. Whereas in the formal garden you can see the backbone of the garden as part of the pattern, in informal gardens the underlying framework is almost entirely disguised by planting and the garden should look as though it has grown up naturally. Nevertheless, some structure needs to exist or everything will relapse into uncontrolled wilderness.

PLANNING FOR INFORMALITY

INFORMAL gardens are more difficult to design than formal ones. Since straight lines and symmetry rule the formal garden, balance is inherent. But the informal garden is ruled by irregularity and natural-looking planting, so the designer must create a balance through a mixture of instinct, experiment and experience. This is rather like painting a picture or like thinking of the garden as a sculpture.

❀ If you are trying to create informality in a plain rectangular plot, consider planning your design on the diagonal. A path might run from the right-hand side near the house, past an oval lawn and end up on the left-hand side at the bottom of the garden. On the way, trees and other planting will create informal screens.

ABOVE: *A medley of shrubs, grasses, fuchsias and low perennial plants make a charmingly informal border next to a large lawn.*

❀ On a sloping site you can create winding or zigzag paths and steps down a grassy bank, rather like the 'flowery mead' of medieval times, planted with bulbs in spring and wild flowers in summer. An irregularly shaped site is made for informal garden planning. You can use awkward spaces for creating secret gardens or for more mundane purposes such as hiding a greenhouse or making a play area.

LEFT: *Bright purples and pinks are easily found in the plant world and always combine well together. The gravel path gives form to what otherwise might be a rather straggling bed.*

Informal shapes

❀ An informal garden has carefully planned spaces but conceals its boundaries. You can create boundaries by using native mixed hedging such as hawthorn, holly and briar roses or, in larger gardens, by planting clumps of trees such as birch or rowan.

❀ Irregularity is achieved by organic-looking spaces and winding curves. A grassy lawn may lead circuitously to a wild garden or a rose garden. Make sure the shapes are generous. Paths should wind gently in large curves, not wiggle up the garden in a worm-like way.

❀ One large curve always looks better than two or three meanly angled ones. Informality implies relaxation, so the whole garden should seem to be relaxed. There should be plenty of space for slow movement around the garden and plenty of places in which to sit.

❀ At each bend a series of tall plants should conceal what is around the corner, so that there is always a new surprise – a flowering cherry tree, a sculpture half-hidden by ivy or a rural arbour – because this should not be a garden with strict patterns, but a garden of random walks and mysteries.

❀ In very narrow plots you can treat the whole garden as a walk, with undulating borders on each side of a gently curving path leading you down to a seat or other eye-catcher at the end. The path can be made of bricks, stone or even grass, although grass is liable to become worn in summer and soggy in winter.

ABOVE: *A narrow border has been filled with plants with strap-like leaves at the back and low-growing perennials at the front. The mosaic pot gives the bed a focal point.*

❀ At intervals on either side of the path, set back into the planting, you can create seating areas, allowing the visitor to pause in their garden walk and enjoy the plants. The plants themselves should be chosen for their colour and scent and they should have interest most of the year. The occasional small tree or large shrub will provide shade and height.

RIGHT: *Even a very small garden can be made to seem larger and be filled with surprises by introducing winding curves, diagonal lines and tall plants to conceal what might be waiting round the corner. Here, a lawn is located fairly near the house and a herb garden at the bottom of the garden; comfortable seats invite the visitor to sit and enjoy the plants.*

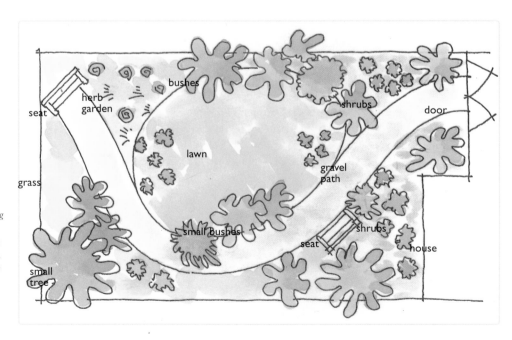

ABOVE: *If your garden lacks tall trees or bushes, add something to bring height and interest into it, such as a planted obelisk.*

Vertical elements

✿ Vertical elements in the garden create a necessary extra dimension and should be added into any planting scheme if possible. They provide interest, 'punctuation points', contrast with spreading plants and mark the ends of avenues. Used in pairs striking vertical plants can become frames to a wider view or gateways to other parts of the garden.

✿ In general, planting in informal gardens will include tall shrubs to create compartments and secret walkways. You will also need the input of taller trees to add to the vertical dimension and to provide shade. They will also hide the edges of the plot, and nearby buildings, and help give a secluded country feeling.

✿ Sculptures, obelisks and other ornamental features can all add a vertical element to a low planting scheme. Obelisks can be more prominently positioned while statues can lurk secretively behind mysterious foliage.

RIGHT: *An informal garden plan means the gardener can revel in an explosion of bright colours. Here, bright pink and red tulips clash merrily with yellow pansies and blue forget-me-nots.*

Flowers for the informal garden

✿ The informal garden revels in colour. Where the formal garden often looks best restricted to a variety of shades of green or green and white, the informal garden may revel in the riotous reds and pinks of pelargoniums and busy Lizzies (*Impatiens*), in nasturtiums, red salvias and sunflowers.

✿ Alternatively, you may choose silvers, pinks and soft blues. These are all colours that respond so well to a paler sun and a misty atmosphere. An informal rose garden should be filled with old-fashioned roses, sharing the space with complementary plants such as foxgloves, lavender and herbaceous clematis. The most important thing about an informal planting scheme is that the garden should have a natural look, as though all the planting had happened of its own accord.

Focal points

✿ Informal gardens do not have the straight walks and avenues that create obvious places for focal points. Their curves and hidden spaces should reveal eye-catching surprises at the last minute. As you round a corner, you should be confronted by something to please, astonish or amuse.

✿ Sculptures should have a sense of movement; this is why animal sculptures often work well. How you place these eye-catchers is all-important because, as they will probably be approached from many different directions, they must look good from all angles. Sculptures will enhance wherever they are situated: they can be hidden behind foliage, hung from the branch of a tree or placed beside a pool or pond.

A feeling of movement

❀ You can control the way people move around your garden by the way you plan the spaces. Long, narrow paths will encourage people to walk fairly quickly. If you want people to linger and look, you must provide wide paths of firm, dry material and seats for them along the way.

❀ A path next to a summer border should be wide enough for two people to linger and admire together, whereas a path going to a compost heap can be narrow and hedged. Paths that are too long, narrow and enclosed will make people feel uncomfortable – the higher the sides, the narrower and longer a path will seem.

A feeling of balance

❀ Balance in the formal garden is provided by symmetry. In an informal garden you have to create your own balance. A large, open space such as a lawn can be balanced by a strong upright tree or sculpture.

❀ A white seat, always a very prominent feature, can be balanced by a dark green background or by setting it in an arbour. A group of trees or shrubs can be balanced by an answering bulk of some kind, such as a table and chairs of a strong defined sculptural shape or a small building.

Water

❀ Natural-looking ponds and pools are ideal water features in informal gardens. You will probably get a better shape by digging the hole and lining it with butyl rather than by buying a preformed liner. Planting should include water plants, as well as marginal and bog plants.

ABOVE: *An intriguing and attractive scheme of mound-shaped flowering plants backed by tall spiky plants and, behind that again, a wall of climbing roses. The colours are predominantly red with shades of yellow, and the neutralising white burns in the middle.*

❀ Other water features could include a small stream or a rocky cascade, which can quite easily be created with a collection of rocks, a small reservoir and a submersible pump. Cobble, millstone and wall fountains can all be useful when you want to provide the sight and sound of water without giving up space to a pond.

ABOVE: *A bright, colourful flowerbed containing – among others –* Calendula, Ligularia, *lilies, delphiniums and roses.*

MATERIALS

GRAVEL is a good material for informal gardens. Concrete slabs set in grass or gravel provide a firm basis for wheelchairs or smart shoes. Bark is good for winding through woodland and will provide a soft landing for children if laid thickly under their play equipment.

ROMANTIC GARDENS

The romantic garden is basically a dream – a garden of bowers and gazebos, of scent and pastel colour, where plants grow with soft, arching habits and sweet-smelling flowers that never outgrow their allotted spaces. Birds flit from branch to branch, ferny foliage is reflected in still pools and nearby are the sounds of waterfalls. The sun shines down on flowers of many colours growing in profusion, never clashing, never dominating, and nobody ever seems to do any actual gardening. Pictures of the flowery enclosures of the Middle Ages depict lovers meeting under apple trees and sitting on turf or camomile seats, while gazing tenderly into each other's eyes.

ABOVE: *A bench or other seat tucked into a small corner of the garden, or in a shady arbour surrounded with sweet-scented flowers, will create a perfect romantic hideaway.*

COLOUR AND SCENT

THERE is no reason why we cannot have a romantic garden in a modern setting. The most important things are colour and scent. The colours should be soft and gentle; pale pink, buff and white are romantic colours, and the flowers should be prolific. There are many new and old roses with pretty colours and delightful scents, which will flower for long periods and will not outgrow their spaces.

❀ Gazebos, garden buildings, arbours and seats with rounded arches or Gothic, pointed 'ogee' shapes are all easy to come by in garden centres. Scented flowers can be grown next to seats and walkways and scented climbers can surround shady arbours.

❀ Shrub roses with good colour and scent include 'Gertrude Jekyll' with rich pink blooms, 'Constance Spry' whose clear pink flowers continue over a long period, 'Buff Beauty' and 'Felicia'. Climbers and ramblers include 'New Dawn', a light satiny pink rose that will grow over a north wall, and 'Albertine', a popular rose with very pretty dark red buds, warm pink flowers and fierce thorns.

THE VICTORIAN ROMANTIC GARDEN

THE modern idea of a romantic garden follows a Victorian tradition. The Victorians were not only interested in the new plants being imported from all over the world, but they found the idea of the strange countries the plants came from wonderfully romantic, too.

BELOW: *This little garden is full of surprises, including the statuette peeping out underneath the rose-covered pergola.*

❀ The larger Victorian garden might include a garden devoted to roses of all kinds, including old scented roses; there were also rockeries, streams and ferneries. Then there was the so-called 'cottage garden', portrayed in idealised watercolours by nineteenth-century artists, showing cheerfully chaotic beds of rampant perennial and annual flowers, growing cheek by jowl in front of thatched cottages.

TODAY'S ROMANTIC GARDEN

MODERN gardeners are highly imaginative and creative when thinking up romantic gardens that can look natural and still be manageable. Traditionally, the orchard is an important part of the idea of a romantic garden, but the idea is symbolic, of course, and there is no need to have rows of fruit trees. One apple tree, two fruit bushes espaliered against a wall or a 'hedge' of cordoned fruit trees will serve the same purpose and be a marvellous addition to your garden.

ABOVE: *Roses are the most exquisite of flowers, whether they are in bud or full bloom. If adequately fed and watered, many will continue to flower until well into autumn or later.*

❀ There are plenty of plants whose common names can give an indication of how romantic a garden was in the old days. Heartsease was the name for the purple and yellow viola. Black-eyed Susan, bachelor's button, love-in-a-mist, forget-me-not, sweet Alison, sweet Cicely and blue-eyed Mary are all names used for cottage garden flowers, many of which are still enchanting planted in natural or romantic gardens.

❀ Today's romantic gardens are liable to be more deliberately designed, with fewer varieties of plants and an easy maintenance bias, but scent and colour and a sense of timelessness are the essence of this style and these things are as attainable today as they ever have been.

LEFT: *The romantic garden is based on curves. Here, a camomile lawn has stepping stones for a path. Its pond is designed to attract wildlife. The pergola is covered with attractive vines, and from the seat you can see the only slightly formal element: a hexagonal summer house as a focal point at the far end.*

island

small tree

summerhouse

pond

camomile lawn

pergola with vine

informal border

paving pathway

seat

door to house

COLOUR IN THE ROMANTIC GARDEN

COLOUR depends so much on where, when and how it is seen. In the romantic garden colour is one of the most important aspects of the planting, so choose plants carefully to look their best in a particular part of the garden. Make sure you design the garden not just to be seen from the house, but to be enjoyed as you walk through or sit in a shady bower. Many plants are best seen close up so provide plenty of seating areas and plant for the pleasure of sitting in these spots.

✤ Dark, rich colours such as purples and reds, and especially deep reds, are exciting when viewed close up with the light behind you. These colours, which include deep red roses and the crimsons, scarlets and loud pinks of pelargoniums, are best kept near the house. Pale colours look best from a distance and these are the

ones most suitable to the romantic style of garden. The pale blue clematis such as 'Lasurstern' and 'Perle d'Azur' are the most effective of all clematis colours in the romantic garden. The deep, rich 'Royal Velours', 'Ville de Lyon' and 'Niobe' clematises are best kept near the house, although the smaller-flowered *viticella* types with their pagoda-shaped flowers can be grown among paler-coloured roses in the main garden very effectively.

✤ Note whether the plants are best seen with the light behind you or behind the plants. The yellow forms of privet (*Ligustrum*), *Philadelphus coronarius* 'Aureus' and *Choisya ternata* 'Sundance' all look best against a dark background and against a north-facing wall. The high sunlight coming over on to the foliage will highlight the yellow beautifully against a dark wall or hedge.

TRADITIONAL PLANTS FOR THE ROMANTIC GARDEN

THERE are many plants that can add to the romantic quality of your garden. During the nineteenth century at least two dozen varieties of vines or wall grapes were grown as ornamental as well as productive plants. Walls were thickly covered with roses. Large colourful flowers were popular, such as peonies and oriental poppies. Scented flowers are an absolute essential in a romantic garden today, for example honeysuckles, lilies and old-fashioned pinks like the clove-scented white 'Mrs Sinkins'.

Climbing roses

✤ Repeat-flowering climbers are the most suitable roses for training up garden arches and bowers, whereas the vigorous but once-flowering ramblers may need the more substantial support of pergolas. 'Aloha' is one of the best repeat-flowering climbing roses, which will eventually grow to 3 m (10 ft). It is very healthy with lovely rich pink fragrant flowers and can be grown quite satisfactorily as a shrub. 'Golden Showers' is a good one if you like yellow. It is almost thornless but does not have much scent. 'New Dawn' is a beautiful pearly pink, highly fragrant and flowers almost continuously. 'Madame Alfred Carrière' is another almost thornless rose with white scented flowers and satisfactory repeat flowering. It will grow on a north-facing wall.

LEFT: *The top of this informal arch is almost completely hidden, as though it were wearing a bonnet of brightly coloured roses.*

ABOVE: *A hammock slung under a tree, surrounded by a summer border with sweet-smelling flowers such as stock, makes a truly romantic environment.*

❀ Rambler roses have only one flowering period, which begins about midsummer. They are easier to train than climbers and the flowers are smaller. They are very vigorous and may be difficult to accommodate in a small garden but worth a try if you have a pergola or wall or even an old tree for them to climb. 'Goldfinch' is a strongly scented pale yellow rose, which grows to a height of 3 m (10 ft).

Old roses

❀ Some of the old Bourbon and Portland roses are very desirable and exactly right for the romantic garden, offering billowing masses of soft colour and elegant habits of growth. Most of the old roses are exquisitely scented. 'Mme Isaac Perrière' is a Bourbon with exceedingly fragrant flowers with fully double globular cups and is said to be the most strongly scented of all roses. It can reach 2 m (7 ft) so make sure you allow it plenty of room.

❀ 'Mme Pierre Oger' also has deeply scented globular flowers of pale silvery pink and an arching habit, one of the most beautiful of all roses. 'La Reine Victoria' has a rather lax habit and may need some support. It has beautifully scented globular flowers, which open pale pink and deepen in colour on exposure to light.

LEFT: *With so many different roses to choose from you will be sure to find a variety to suit your garden, whatever the size, aspect or shape. Include roses in your romantic garden to add both colour and scent.*

WILDLIFE GARDENS

As with all gardens, in a wildlife garden you are not attempting to re-create nature itself, but designing a garden in which native species of plants, birds and animals will flourish. A wildlife garden can be used for human enjoyment as well. It can look well designed and modern without losing any of its attraction to small creatures, who don't mind whether it looks rural and 'natural' and just want the plants and habitats they can feel at home with. If the soil near the house is filled with builders' rubble, you can cover it with decking. This will be useful as a 'patio' and also for observing the garden from a slight height.

WILDLIFE HABITATS

WILDLIFE can be enticed into the garden by providing a variety of habitats and sources of food. Ideally, the garden should contain a woodland area, a wild flower meadow and a pond, all features that can be adapted to fit into a small garden successfully. Make the most of the conditions that prevail in your garden. For example, a poor soil is ideal for growing a wild flower meadow, while a damp, shady area will suit many woodland plants.

❀ Other good habitats include a pond and a dry stone wall or a pile of logs. You need plants that will supply pollen, nectar, berries and seeds. Wild flowers will also encourage many small creatures. Give structure to the garden with a natural stone path set in grass or a forest bark path winding through a grove of trees. A slightly raised seating area will give a view over the garden. Surround it with a planting of tall shrubs so that it will offer opportunities for watching small creatures as they move around in your garden.

Planting

❀ You can apply the same ground rules for the design of this type of garden as with any other: creating well-proportioned garden spaces, focal points, areas of interest and varied planting.
❀ A sunny flowerbed is the perfect place for growing some of the old cornfield weeds such as corncockle, corn marigold, cornflowers and poppies. A mixture of poppies alone makes a really spectacular sight in the middle of summer.
❀ If you have a fairly large garden, you might like a central meadow with wild flowers and grass seed

ABOVE: *A wild meadow in England with yellow daisies, cornflowers, oregano and many different grasses.*

BELOW: *The spectacular sight of a meadow planted with wild flowers in France. Seen here are cornflowers, poppies and daisies, making an astonishing splash of colour.*

appropriate to the soil type. Choose a part of the garden that has rather poor soil if possible. Unlike most garden plants, wild flowers need soil with low fertility. This will help to restrict the more vigorous grasses so that the wild flowers have a chance to compete. Remove any turf and topsoil and replace it with subsoil.

❀ Buy an inexpensive kit for testing the soil so that you know its pH, and buy a mixture of wild flowers seeds that will grow well on that. There are several seed companies selling appropriate mixtures. The plants should come into flower at roughly the same time, either all in spring or all in summer, so that you can cut the grass when appropriate. A spring-flowering meadow should be cut in midsummer and then mowed as usual until autumn or cut once again in late autumn. A summer-flowering meadow should be cut once in late spring and then again in late autumn.

❀ A true lawn will have its own wildlife community, too. Do not allow dandelions and plantain in, but you can add seed of white clover to the lawn seed or scatter it on to an existing lawn. You can mow a path through this meadow and around its edges so it is easy to walk round and admire the flowers.

ABOVE: *The cheerful little marigold* Calendula officinalis *will fill gaps in the summer garden and associates well with many different flowers.*

BELOW: *A wildlife garden implies a certain amount of laissez-faire. Do not try to keep it too neat. A small heap of sticks and prunings may encourage hedgehogs, for example. A pond with overgrown edges will encourage other small creatures to run back and forth. A woodland section will attract squirrels and birds and if you have a boggy area, you can grow a wider variety of plants.*

BELOW: *Treating the garden as a wildlife sanctuary means allowing flowers to retain their seed heads. Here,* Agapanthus *seed heads create interesting structural shapes.*

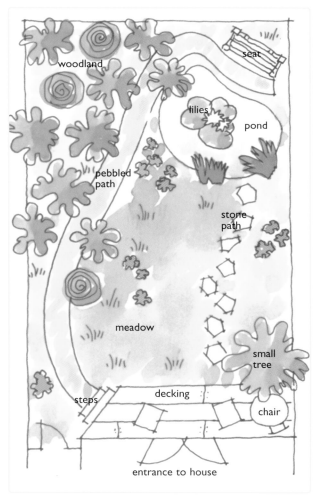

woodland

seat

lilies

pond

pebbled path

stone path

meadow

small tree

steps

decking

chair

entrance to house

Woodland

❀ A woodland edge provides a rich natural habitat for wildlife and may attract hedgehogs, bats and a range of other wild creatures. You can re-create this sort of environment even on a small scale to bring a greater diversity of creatures into the garden. A woodland area should consist of several layers of vegetation, including tall trees, smaller trees and a lower tier of shrubs. Under these can be planted smaller ground-cover plants and early bulbs.

❀ In a small garden, where large trees such as English oak (*Quercus ruber*) and beech (*Fagus sylvatica*) would not be appropriate, plant hazel (*Corylus avellana*), hawthorn (*Crataegus*) or bird cherry (*Prunus padus*), all of which will support wildlife. In a small town garden, use a mixed hedge as the top layer or substitute climbing plants including woodbine (*Lonicera periclymenum*) grown up a trellis. Small shrubs for the intermediate layer could include *berberis* and cotoneaster. Plants such as wood spurge (*Euphorbia amygdaloides*) and wood sorrel (*Oxalis acetosella*), which enjoy damp, shady situations, are good plants to grow in woodland.

❀ Every wildlife garden needs a pond as a home for all sorts of animal, bird and insect life and this should be in the most open area of the garden. It will make an

ABOVE: *A variety of trees and dense ground cover using ivies, hostas and ferns make this a most attractive woodland walk.*

excellent focal point. Boggy and marginal plants will make a natural-looking surround and offer cover for smaller wild creatures.

Windbreaks

❀ Fences provide inexpensive instant windbreaks. They can be of woven willow or hazel, or even of wattle for a medieval look. All of these are all good at gently filtering the wind. Since this is an organic garden you will want to dedicate an area to composting, hidden by shrubs or a hedge or fencing to match that used in the rest of the garden.

❀ Hedges provide food, shelter, nesting sites and a safe, sheltered corridor for travelling creatures. Choose a flowering hedge such as *Rosa rugosa* 'Frau Dagmar Hastrup', which is a pretty pale pink, or the pure white 'Blanche Double de Coubert'. Alternatively, plump for clipped holly or a mixed hedge. Conifers do not mix well with other evergreen shrubs and do not make the best wildlife hedges on their own.

LEFT: *A woodland area can be one of the most attractive parts of a garden, as shown here by the graceful shape and autumn colour of this small* Acer japonicum.

Shrubs for a mixed hedge

❀ Choose one species as the mainstay of the hedge. The common hawthorn (*Crataegus monogyna*) is an attractive choice, with its sprays of fragrant white flowers in spring, red leaves and purple haws in autumn. The blackthorn (*Prunus spinosa*) is another good mainstay hedging plant, with its white flowers in spring and blue-black sloes in autumn.

❀ Choose from the following to interplant with your main choice: buckthorn (*Rhamnus catharticus*), which provides food for the caterpillar of the brimstone butterfly; holly (*Ilex aquifolium*); dogwood (*Cornus sanguinea*); wild privet (*Ligustrum vulgare*), which has strongly scented white flowers in summer; hazel (*Corylus avellana*), with pretty dangling catkins; and spindle (*Euonymus europaeus*) which has extraordinary puce and orange berries, beloved by birds.

Variety is the spice of wildlife

❀ The best garden for wildlife is one with the most variety of plants. A bit of grass, some herbaceous plants, some roses, some vegetables, a tree or two, even a few weeds such as nettles and a privet that some caterpillars need to feed on, will make a good start. The garden borders should be wide enough to take several layers of vegetation.

ABOVE: *These cherry trees allow useful ground-cover plants such as honesty and periwinkle to carpet the ground beneath them.*

ABOVE: *If you provide the right woodland conditions you may get hedgehogs visiting your garden. They should be welcomed, since they eat slugs and snails.*

❀ Make sure there are some evergreen shrubs for winter cover as well as winter interest, and some deciduous trees and shrubs to let some light through in the spring. Each layer of vegetation provides a habitat for different creatures. Thrushes are at home in the tree tops, sparrows and tits congregate slightly lower down, and blackbirds like to peck around and listen for worms on the ground. Spiders, beetles and mice will all make their homes in a pile of stones in a secluded corner.

Birdlife

- Birds can be encouraged to nest in the garden if you fix nesting boxes to the trees. Put these up in autumn or midwinter so the birds have time to go house hunting and explore them thoroughly before the next nest-building season begins.
- Nesting boxes with small holes (about 3 cm or 1¼ in) will allow smaller birds such as nuthatches and tits to use them. Larger entrance holes will attract a wider range of birds. A box should be fixed high enough so that cats and squirrels cannot reach it. The positioning is crucial. It should be sheltered from wind, rain and strong sunlight and away from bird tables.
- Birds are attracted by such plants as asters, golden rod, cornflowers, teazel, cotoneasters, violas, fennel, lavender, forget-me-nots, scabious, sorbus, honeysuckle and pyracantha. Insects enjoy *Phacelia tanacetifolia*, a hardy annual with bell-shaped blue flowers with prominent stamens, which seeds itself around the garden even in poor soils. Insects also like thyme, mint, oregano, crocuses and ivy.

ABOVE: *A thoughtful gardener has created a colourful spring-flowering garden at the edge of a wood where it meets the road.*

BELOW: *Soft greens and the palest of yellows provide colour and texture in a border between a meadow lawn and a hedge.*

Butterfly borders

- Butterflies like to sunbathe in sunny, sheltered spots that are protected from the wind. In a perennial border grow *Aubrieta* to attract painted ladies, red admirals, brimstones and small tortoiseshell butterflies. The same butterflies use lavender as a nectar source, as do the small copper, common blue, meadow brown and small skipper. Later in the year they will be attracted by Michaelmas daisies (*Aster*), valerian (*Centranthus*), phlox and *Sedum spectabile*, which has fleshy green leaves and flattish heads of tiny pink flowers in late summer and autumn. It has thin narrow florets, into which the butterflies can reach for nectar with their long tongues.
- Honesty has heads of small purple flowers and is a good source of food for caterpillars of the orange-tip butterfly, and the lilac- or white-flowered buddlejas are well known for attracting peacock and tortoiseshell butterflies, which can absolutely cover the flowers on a sunny day.

Other insects

- Flowers are attractive to bees for both their nectar and pollen and they are also important as a continuous food larder from early spring to late autumn. Particular favourites are herbs such as thyme, marjoram, mint, lavender and lemon balm.
- Beneficial insects in the garden pollinate fruit and vegetables and prey on common garden pests. Between them, anthocorid bugs, ladybirds, hoverflies, lacewings, ground beetles and centipedes will eat caterpillars, midges, weevils, scale insects and red spider mites, slugs, snails, mealy bugs, thrips, scale insects, leafhoppers, aphids and cabbage fly and carrot root fly eggs and larvae. So choosing plants that will attract the beneficial insects is obviously sensible. Fennel (*Foenciulum vulgare*), with its flat heads of yellow

flowers above feathery leaves, is a favourite plant of hoverflies. Pollen and nectar-feeding insects also love sunflowers (*Helianthus annuus*).

✿ Other useful flowers are the annual pot marigolds (*Calendula officinalis*), the poached egg flower

ABOVE: Gleditsia *trees and* Linaria *provide contrasting colours on the edge of a wooded area.*

(*Limnanthes douglasii*), Californian poppy (*Eschscholtzia californica*), baby blue eyes (*Nemophila*), yarrow (*Achillea*), anaphalis, Shasta daisy (*Chrysanthemum maximum*), sea holly (*Eryngium*), wild strawberry (*Fragaria vesca*) and candytuft (*Iberis*).

Preference for species plants

✿ When choosing flowers remember that single flowers are best if you want to encourage wildlife to visit your garden. The extra petals in double forms are often formed at the expense of nectaries and anthers, which means they provide less food for insects. For example, the common bird's foot trefoil has a yellow pea flower, which produces plenty of nectar, but the double variety has none at all.

✿ In other plants, the extra petals on double flowers often make an insurmountable barrier for insects. This means that often they cannot get into the flower to find the food at all.

✿ You need to check that nasturtium and columbine flowers have pointed sacs (or spurs) behind the flowers. These are reservoirs for nectar and are important for species like long-tongued bumble bees, an increasingly threatened form of wildlife.

✿ Delphiniums and larkspurs should also have spurs. When in doubt, choose old-fashioned varieties of plant and the nearest to the wild flower or species as possible. They are often more graceful and elegant in any case.

✿ Night-flowering nectar plants include flowering tobacco (*Nicotiana alata*) and night-scented stock (*Matthiola longipetala*). These will attract night-flying insects, which in turn may attract bats.

ABOVE: A decorative Rodgersia *stands out against a background of ferns in woodland.*

PLANNED GARDENS

❦

Planned gardens are precise and often arranged symmetrically around a central axis, which divides the garden down the middle. The central path may have paths crossing it at right angles, dividing the garden into rectangles or squares. A very small and square garden might not have a straight path, just a central feature with paving around it. The positive symmetrical shapes of the garden must be kept very defined and clear. Paths should be carefully detailed, hedges precise and evergreen shrubs clipped into disciplined shapes. Several features have been associated with the great formal gardens of early times. Many can be introduced into small gardens with great success. The style is particularly suitable for square or rectangular level sites where the symmetry fits well into the basic shape of the plot.

Hedges

❀ Because a symmetrical pattern is the important thing, hedges are often used to mark out the pattern like piping on a cushion. Many of these are low so that they emphasise the basic geometry and do not hide one part from another. Box is one of the most popular shrubs for low hedges, as it grows slowly and is easy to clip into attractive shapes.

❀ Tall, clipped hedges of yew, privet, hornbeam or beech can create divisions between different areas or mark out the perimeter. Straight avenues can be lined on either side by pleached hornbeam or lime. Pleaching means planting the trees equal distances apart, cutting off the lower branches and intertwining or grafting the side branches to meet at about eye level, making a

ABOVE: *An attractive paved path dividing up a small garden can work well when there is a symmetrical planting scheme on both sides of the path.*

clipped hedge on tall 'stalks'. In larger gardens two rows can be planted to create a dense double hedge with a tunnel in the middle.

Knots and parterres

❀ Knot gardens were popular in Tudor times and were based on ancient mazes. These developed into small, rectangular, intricate geometric patterns planted in a continuous, unbroken line. A knot garden may be complete in itself or filled with colours to accentuate

LEFT: *Simple geometrical parterres can enhance any garden – no matter how small.*

LEFT: *A small garden showing careful attention to planting, precise patterning in the terracing and formal placing of garden furniture.*

triangles, hexagons and octagons. This need not necessarily mean straight lines. An oval shape can be very satisfactory in a rectangular plot and circular shapes have often been used very successfully inside square plots.

❀ Adjacent shapes can touch, overlap or be separated by a gap. It is usually best to choose one shape, such as a square, and then arrange squares of different size in a formal pattern.

Axis paths

❀ When making your axis lines, you can reinforce them by planting clipped hedges along each side. Box is the most popular for this but lavender or rosemary will also make attractive low hedges. If you want something taller, plant standard roses on supports.

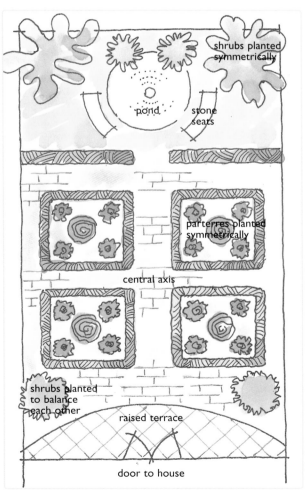

the shapes. Traditionally, different coloured gravels and coal or perhaps low-growing herbs such as thyme and lavender were used. Today recycled glass chippings and coloured glass pebbles have added to the possibilities.

❀ A parterre is simpler than a knot – often planted in individual squares, not joined up together. Parterres were developed from knots in 17th-century France where they were designed to be viewed from first-floor windows. They are usually larger and more open and the plants grown inside them can be taller, for example shrub roses such as 'Felicia', 'Ballerina' and 'Iceberg'. Parterres can also be used for growing vegetables.

Symmetrical shapes

❀ Symmetrical shapes are those that are regular in outline. Although squares, rectangles and circles are the most common shapes, it is also possible to use

RIGHT: *This garden leads, via two steps, from a curved patio of square slabs to four squares of clipped yew set in brick paving. Each square has a standard small rose or bay tree in the center. A clipped hedge divides this area from a circular pond with seats for peaceful contemplation.*

ABOVE: *The wooden garden chair provides a focal point here, with the eye being drawn from the herringbone-patterned paving by the symmetry of the carefully clipped bushes on either side of the seat.*

BELOW: *Geometrically shaped beds of box make up this parterre. They are divided by narrow brick paths and filled with a variety of white flowers, mainly with silver leaves.*

Vertical elements

❀ Because so much of the pattern in planned gardens is derived from paths and low hedges, it is necessary to bring in some vertical elements to provide height and interest and break up all the straight lines. These elements can be introduced in various ways. An attractive sundial or bird bath on a pedestal or a stone fountain can make a good central feature and eyecatcher. Yew or box clipped into tall shapes or mop-headed box or bay trees in tubs can be positioned in rows on either side of a path.

Focal points

❀ A focal point is something that attracts attention. It might be a small building or tree on the horizon or a sculpture or urn. A focal point should be placed deliberately. You do not want the eye attracted towards a washing line or tool shed, for example. The eye likes to go to a focal point in a straight line, so formal gardens are asking for focal points to be positioned at the ends of straight paths and avenues.

❀ A focal point can be anything, from a specimen tree, to a well-designed bench in an arbour, a small summer house or a white painted seat (the colour white acts as an instant focal point).

❀ A view could also be a focal point. To do this you will need to frame it with planting or create a 'window' in a clipped hedge through which to see it.

Materials

❀ Formal style is highly disciplined. Paving materials need to be very carefully chosen so that they are in sympathy with any nearby buildings. Even mixing different kinds and colours of bricks can produce a disruptive effect.

❀ All materials should be well defined. It is best to use as few materials as possible so that the overall effect gives a sense of unity. If using paving stones, they should be placed in a geometric manner, not as crazy paving, which is seldom suited to a formal plan.

❀ When laying bricks you will find that a herringbone pattern has a softer effect than when the bricks are laid in straight lines. Paths can be edged with small cobbles to give them an 'outline' to reinforce the pattern. Both brick and stone make a warm, static ground cover that marries well with brick walls to give a unified design.

❀ Gravel is not usually a good choice for the symmetrical garden. It is too easily kicked around and does not provide a clear enough outline for the geometric garden. One exception is a very small garden that is more for viewing than for walking around, where gravel can make an effective background for a central clipped shrub or stone sculpture.

Water

❀ Water is very much part of the traditional formal garden. It harks back to the desert gardens of old with their irrigation channels and refreshing central pools.

❀ A central pool of circular or geometric shape, perhaps with a fountain in the centre, or indeed any central water feature with a symmetrical shape will look in place.

❀ Narrow channels can run alongside paths and long, rectangular ponds with matching seats on either side will enable visitors to sit and enjoy water lilies and the reflections of the sky. A long, narrow rectangular pond can have a fountain at each end to add interest.

❀ If water is the central element in the garden, it creates an atmosphere of great tranquillity. The reflecting quality of the water in a large pool, plus pale-coloured paving, will give the centre of the garden a very light, optimistic feeling.

❀ The pool should of course be symmetrical and balanced. In an enclosed area, more water can be added via wall fountains. Even water plants can be placed symmetrically.

❀ A wide paved path allows the visitor to get near the water, and steps can lead right down to the water's edge. A symmetrical row of small trees or a clipped hedge will act as a framework to the pool, giving a general feeling of privacy and accentuating the formality.

CHILDREN IN THE PLANNED GARDEN

THERE is no reason why young children should not be able to play in a formal garden. Clipped hedges are usually pretty sturdy, particularly in tubs, and the very fact of having paved paths and straight lines means that running and cycling, roller-skating and skate-boarding are made possible. Remember that paths should be wide enough to make all these activities easy and it is a good idea to provide turning circles at each end.

RIGHT: *Graded heights make these yew topiary shapes very intriguing. Combined with the red standard roses and the white shrub rose, they make an impressive sight.*

SMALL GARDENS

The key to the formal garden is repetition, unity and geometrical patterns and spaces. Small square or rectangular gardens belonging to urban houses are well suited to formality. The symmetrical shape is good for the geometric division of spaces and for straight lines of plants. Remember that although clipped hedges are a highly finished kind of formality, the mere lining out of identical plants in rows is in itself a formal arrangement. Designs can be based on ancient or modern models.

A Persian garden

❦ The first pleasure gardens in Egypt and Persia were based on water and their long narrow canals ran in grid patterns, stemming from the idea of the four-square paradise garden. Where these channels met, there would be a large central pond or tank with fish and water lilies. The royal paradise garden was large, with raised pavilions to catch the slightest breeze. Here you could sit under the shade of trees and enjoy the sound of running water and the scents and colours of flowers.

❦ Although in temperate areas water does not have quite the same significance as it does in desert areas, we still find water soothing and relaxing. Most gardens, large or small, are more interesting if they include a pool, fountain or stream. In city gardens an enclosed garden designed along Persian lines can keep ugly neighbouring buildings out of sight. Even in tiny gardens a narrow channel of water can be created, either running alongside a path or taking up the centre of the plot.

❦ Narrow flower-beds can run around the perimeter with seats or spaces for sitting under shady trees. In a small garden you can use paths rather than water as your grid with some formal planting on either side of standard rose bushes and clipped shapes in box or yew. Fastigiate (having erect branches) and mop-headed trees will provide shade without taking up too much light.

A Moorish garden

❦ There are many similarities between Persian and Moorish gardens, for example the shady trees, scented flowers and the idea of water channels. But whereas Persian gardens were enclosed to keep out the desert, in Moorish gardens the rigid and confined lines were opened up to give splendid views of orchards, olive groves and distant hills.

❦ Patios, porticos and arcades made an almost seamless transition between the house and the garden. Similarly, the wall or hedge of your four-square garden could open out to reveal a tree or an interesting piece of architecture outside the garden itself. Columned summer houses can give a cloister-like impression.

LEFT: A very small space can be given interest by the pots used. Here, a pair of chimney pots has been planted with clipped box, giving a striking and unusual appearance. The box leaves serve to echo the green of the door.

Box-edged borders

✿ An elaborate parterre may be too large for the smaller garden but simpler box-edged borders are very suitable. Although the plants may take some time to get going, they will eventually form a solid block of foliage that is a good foil to other plants. The variegated varieties, although pretty, do not create such a good background and are best grown as features on their own.

LEFT: *Simple borders – such as this carefully laid out lavender border, with its attractive cloche at the centre – are often best for a small garden.*

BELOW: *Formality can be achieved with repetition, unity and geometric lines. A small fountain in the middle is surrounded by a low hedge and a perimeter of grass, the width of a lawn mower. Formal seats are set in niches created by clipped yew hedges and sheltered by topiary shapes.*

A parterre

✿ The parterre is basically a 'flat' pattern, often best seen from a height, such as a first-floor window or a raised terrace or mount. In fact, it was designed to be seen by ladies upstairs in grand houses. Even where there is no raised area, a parterre can still be enjoyed while walking through it. It may be part of a larger formal garden or can take up the whole of a small garden.

✿ The simplest parterre, perhaps a rectangle or square of clipped box or shrubby honeysuckle such as *Lonicera nitida*, makes an excellent design for a small front garden, which is usually viewed in passing, rather than actually entered. In this way the parterre can be designed to have immediate impact on the passerby and the plants in it can be chosen with this in mind.

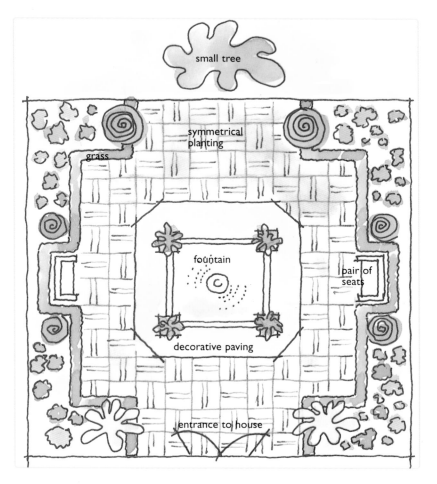

small tree

symmetrical planting

grass

fountain

pair of seats

decorative paving

entrance to house

FORMAL FRONT GARDENS

A VERY small garden may not offer much scope for an extended symmetrical arrangement but even one small standard tree in a square bed edged with box will make a charming formal front garden. You could place a clipped bay (*Laurus nobilis*) in a tub at each corner of the bed and use paving slabs or gravel as the surrounding material.

❀ If the site is sunny and you do not want the shade of even a small tree, the silvery leaves of the small shrub *Convolvulus cneorum* in a small sea of gravel will look pretty all year round. In a shady area, grow one bold plant of *Hosta sieboldiana*, whose bluey-green leaves are large and important looking.

Clipped hedging plants

❀ Although box is probably the longest-lasting hedging plant, and has very attractive glossy dark-green foliage, there are several others that will make attractive edging hedges and you may prefer the silvery look that many of them offer.

ABOVE: *Careful planting, pruning and clipping of bushes such as bay can introduce a sense of formality into even the smallest of garden areas.*

LEFT: *This tiny, narrow garden incorporates careful planning in the decorative paving work, the small ponds mirroring each other and the planting along the pathway.*

❀ Lavender, rosemary and santolina were all traditionally used as clipped hedging plants and are still very attractive used in this way. They are not as long lasting as box and if you want them to live for many years, they must all be cut back really hard. They do not like to be crowded and hate any competition for light, moisture and nutrients so make sure there is a gap between the hedge and the planting inside it.

Formal but soft

❀ A very long, narrow plot can seem difficult to deal with formally because its ribbon-like shape already accentuates the straight lines and constricted space. To get over this problem, you can soften the lines of straight paths by creating circular areas along the way, planting dome-shaped plants and clipping shrubs into rounded shapes.

ABOVE: *This picturesque old-fashioned thatched cottage is very formal with its neat clipped hedge and white gate. The topiary columns support a clipped shape that echoes the thatching on the roof.*

❀ Similarly, the path can be lined with round-headed flowers. For example, the soft rounded shapes of golden marjoram and alliums, which will produce big round flower heads in summer, are particularly effective. Gravel rather than paving or brick will also soften the outline.

Axes and vistas

❀ One of the first decisions to make is the direction of the main axes. This will determine where the main vistas will lie and the garden's relationship to the house. The ornaments and features that close a vista can be added at a later stage. In most cases you will want the main axis to relate to the main door of the house so that garden and house can be seen as one entity in the plan.

❀ Cross-axes should be at right angles, but this is not always easy to achieve if the ground is not level or the plot not rectangular. At Sissinghurst in Kent the axes are not always at right angles but this has been cleverly concealed by the planting.

Materials

❀ The choice of material for hard surfaces and how it is laid can make or spoil a formal garden. Gravel is a versatile material, which combines well with other surfaces, including concrete and granite setts (paving blocks).

❀ Always get the best quality of any material that you can afford. York stone is unfortunately too expensive for most gardeners but there are acceptable forms of reconstituted stone, which can look perfectly good.

❀ Rounded cobblestones are attractive visually but uncomfortable to walk on, so should be used only for decorative details among other, more solid, paving slabs. Cobblestones are useful as a contrast to other materials and as part of a decorative paving pattern. They can also be used to mark transitions between two separate areas or the change of direction of a path. Tiles or bricks laid on their edges can also mark changes of direction or provide interesting edging between other materials.

Plants for formal gardens

❀ Edging plants are useful for emphasising the line of a straight border. Choose those that will be of interest over a long season and use one plant along the whole length of the border to give a sense of unity. Possible plants include *Alchemilla mollis*, a pretty greeny-yellow plant that associates well with almost everything and has a nice tumbling habit.

❀ The catmint *Nepeta cataria* is another good edging plant if your border is wide enough to accommodate it. *Bergenia cordifolia*, otherwise known as elephant's ears, will give a border a striking dark green edging, which turns red in autumn.

CONTEMPORARY GARDENS

❦

Many modern buildings have simple, rectangular shapes, repetitive forms and the minimum of applied decoration. It is the shape of the whole structure that is important – the spacing and proportion of windows and doors and the relationship of the different planes. To complement such buildings, we need to design gardens of great simplicity, elegance and style, which will reflect the geometric lines of the house with their own geometric lines, softened by planting.

MODERNIST IDEAS

MODERNIST principles in gardening come from the Modernist style of architecture, which emerged at the beginning of the twentieth century. This made use of the newest technological developments to design buildings that did not have to rely on traditional building techniques. Reinforced concrete could be moulded into exciting new forms, creating lighter buildings with bigger, interconnected spaces and uncluttered interiors.

❦ Today there is a new wave of Modernist thinking, which regards the garden as an outside room whose link with the house is paramount. Key elements of the building's architecture such as doors and windows will be repeated as elements of the garden. Wooden floors inside the house can be repeated outside with wooden decking, and stone floors with stone paving. A lawn or rectangular paved area outside can be related to a rug indoors.

❦ Even if your house is not particularly interesting architecturally, you can feel free to interpret a traditional style in a modern way, bringing new ideas to an old theme. Whereas the classical formal garden is based on a central axis, Modernist gardens are always asymmetrical. Nevertheless, they are unmistakably formal. The lines are geometric, the ideas and plants are few but repeated. The angles and spaces are dynamic, implying energy and life, but the uncluttered terraces are also tranquil.

❦ The trimmings are the plants, which include spring and summer flowers, grown in pots and urns or galvanised metal buckets and dustbins. They can be moved around as desired. Such gardens are designed for minimum maintenance, often for people with busy lives and exacting jobs who want to use the garden for leisure and entertaining, not for propagating and growing. There is no aping nature here; this is an artificial environment and proud of it.

Forms and shapes

❦ All shapes should be simple, functional and unpretentious. If you are designing an exotic garden or one that uses architectural plants, clarity of geometric form is desirable as a balance to the untidiness of plant growth. If you choose to design your garden in the geometric manner, do it confidently.

RIGHT: A tall, curved concrete wall has been painted deep ultramarine and decorated with sea creatures and flying ducks. The mosaic table adds extra colour and interest.

LEFT: *Square containers and a restricted planting scheme will complement many modern gardens. Here, a galvanised container has been filled with bold and colourful plants using only reds and yellows.*

Narrow gardens

✤ The paving in a typically narrow city garden can be done inexpensively with concrete slabs. Along one edge you could cut the concrete to form a generous curve which will leave room for a flowerbed with some depth. This means that at the widest part, you will be able to grow two or three tiers of plants, which will give opportunity for more plant height and variety.

Courtyard gardens

✤ You can modernise the Italianate courtyard style by using a formal pool of water with an elaborate but modern fountain in the centre, surrounded by terra-cotta tiles with brick edging. As for plants, keep to formal, clipped evergreens in very simple containers. Galvanised containers include buckets and dustbins. Just one or two of these planted with architectural palms, for example, will create an outdoor room of great style and panache.

✤ In a small front courtyard, you can paint the walls in any deep colour. The introduction of new ranges of outdoor paints has enabled gardeners to paint fences, walls and whole courtyards in colours that will highlight plant forms and leaves to great effect.

✤ The style will suit any modern building, whether made of concrete, brick or timber, and can be used with modern mock Georgian or other brick houses, especially where the gardens are rather squeezed in between buildings. Often, these oddly shaped plots are asking for a geometric solution to the design.

RIGHT: *The modern garden takes the idea of the garden 'room' quite literally. The lines are geometric, the feeling architectural, the plants few but sculptural. Modern materials such as engineering bricks or decking can be used, and water is often present in the form of a sculptural fountain, again using modern materials such as stainless steel or glass.*

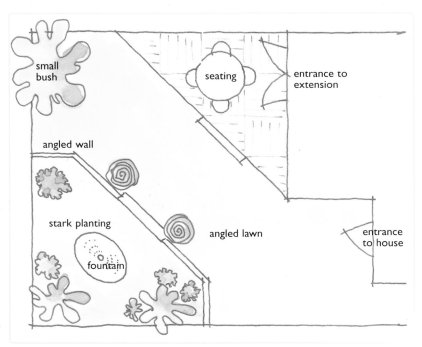

small bush

seating

entrance to extension

angled wall

stark planting

fountain

angled lawn

entrance to house

ABOVE: *In this garden, the owner has painted a curved line on the fence, which leads the eye into the curved line of the actual garden where it turns into woodland.*

Small rectangular gardens

❀ If the garden is very small, you can divide it up diagonally, the long line creating a feeling of more length. Mark the line with a change of level or a change of material, perhaps using gravel for one side and concrete slabs for the other.

Materials

❀ The first consideration in a modern garden is not necessarily the planting. Indeed, there may be very few plants or even none at all. The surfaces of the walls and floors of the garden offer many opportunities for decoration. The traditional garden used mostly brick, stone, granite setts (paving blocks), sand or gravel.

❀ The modern garden designer can add to such materials glazed tiles, mosaic (especially on walls), glass bricks, mirrors, coloured glass beads and rubber and other reconstituted materials. Glass bricks need some support but can be let into suitable frames. There are also bright stainless metal containers, poles and columns, which can be the supports for 'sails' for shade, rather than the traditional garden umbrella.

❀ Traditional materials are often perfectly suitable for the modern garden but used rather differently. Slate can be cut and laid with great precision. Precision cutting suits the spare 'hard-edged' designs of contemporary architecture. Alternatively, it can be sawn in random lengths and laid as a patio, path or surround for a geometrically shaped pool or L-shaped canal.

❀ Green slate is ideal for the modern garden but the surface should be roughened so that it is non-slip in all weathers.

❀ Any paved area should have a unified feeling, and this is especially important to counterbalance any exotic planting.

❀ Timber decking is a good material for many modern gardens, particularly roof gardens. It can look really magnificent with the dark, rough texture of railway sleepers used as retaining walls or with brick and, surprisingly perhaps, it also seems to go very well with modern galvanised containers.

RIGHT: *Modern gardens should be functional and unpretentious. The tall and secure fence of this garden is made of simple wooden poles painted in graded shades of blue and purple.*

❀ Concrete can be coloured with the addition of coloured cements. The various stone colours are usually the most popular because they are the 'kindest' and quietest foil to grass and plants.

Vertical elements

❀ Fine timber laths can create elegant vertical structures such as pergolas with a definitely modern look. They can symbolise tree trunks and create the feeling of a small copse or grove, but are very far removed from the deliberately rustic look of the traditional pergola. They will complement the straight lines of narrow decking. Timber obelisks can take the place of fastigiate trees with their erect branches, such as junipers or yews.

❀ Modern lighting can also add to the vertical effect. Globes on metal 'stems' give a modern effect. The stem can rise up from a group of dome-shaped shrubs, which themselves echo the shade's rounded shape.

Paint

❀ Walls, fences, furniture and containers can all be painted. White reflects more light than any other colour and will brighten a shady wall. It is also a good colour for highlighting foliage shapes.

❀ However, the enormous advances made in outdoor paints and the colour ranges now available give the modern gardener a really exciting choice. Blue-green and grey-green seem to be universally attractive colours in a garden and again, most foliage and flower colours and shapes look well against them. However,

the brightest orange and the deepest blue can look right, too, when used with confidence and minimal planting, and many sculptural objects, particularly abstract ones, can look marvellous against them.

The plants

❀ Plants without flowers are ideally suited to the Modernist garden. Ferns such as *Athyrium filix-femina* can be massed together in front of a large-leaved ivy such as *Hedera helix* 'Montgomery'. Groups of three small trees planted together, such as *Betula pendula*, especially those with interesting bark, will remain small and look attractive. Their lacy foliage and narrow trunks will allow you to see the architecture through them.

❀ Large square or rectangular containers will also relate to the architecture and you can grow exotic plants such as palms, hostas or grasses in them.

Colour

❀ If you do want to introduce colour, it is best to choose restricted colour schemes so that the colour will not detract from the bold lines and geometric spaces of the garden plan. You can plant in blocks of geometric colour using pelargoniums or bedding plants and you can use foliage colour such as the red forms of *Phormium*.

BELOW: *Modern paints are available in a range of colours as bright as garden flowers themselves. Here, panels of a concrete fence have been painted in uninhibited shades of green, red and yellow.*

JAPANESE GARDENS

❦

Japanese gardens have developed over many centuries and have been refined and shaped by religious and philosophical ideas, ranging from Shintoism, Hinduism and Taoism to Buddhism – very different from the classical roots of Christianity and Islam that have shaped European garden traditions. The basic principle behind Japanese gardens is a quest for harmony and an important element is the idea of retaining the spirit of the place and appreciating the beauty of the natural rock.

THE PRINCIPLES

IN early Japanese gardens design principles included the idea that rocks already *in situ* should be respected for their own inner stillness, and that rocks, islands and ponds represented nature and should always be placed asymmetrically. Symmetrical elements represented humans.

❀ The representation of a mountain is essential and refers to the Cosmic Mountain at the centre of the universe. The Island of Immortality can be represented by an island or a rock. Rocks are arranged in groups of three. In old Japanese gardening books this is explained as representing three forces – horizontal, diagonal and vertical – which correspond to the structure of the universe – heaven, earth and humankind.

❀ The aim is not to overpower nature but to enter into a partnership with it. The garden is a place for divine spirits and when harmony is achieved, the good spirits will be drawn into the garden while the hostile ones will leave it in peace.

ABOVE: *This is an unusual but attractive and appropriate way to fence off a Japanese-style garden, using bamboo poles knotted together with rope.*

BELOW: *Bright red fish in a still pond are not difficult to keep, and they coordinate with the red paint used on many Japanese bridges.*

ABOVE: *Japanese design is always very disciplined. The black decking and the single shapely plant in a pot very much reflect the Japanese sense of design.*

❀ Everywhere in the garden there should be devices to ward off evil spirits. Trees and stones should be grouped in odd numbers – threes, fives and sevens. Devils are thought to walk in straight lines so garden pathways are made to twist and turn.

❀ In the Japanese garden non-living features are paramount and plants are not the prime ingredients. One of the most important items is water – the Japanese word for gardener means 'He who makes the bed of streams'. Others are stone, sand, gravel, bamboo, aged trees and space.

❀ There is a 15th-century Japanese diagram that shows how a landscape should be deliberately designed to look natural. It has 16 pieces of land and water arranged around a central 'guardian stone'. The design is asymmetrical but carefully balanced, and each piece has a distinct function and importance. The pieces include mountains (near and far), rocks, beaches, islands, a lake and a cascade.

❀ Every item is balanced by something else. Tall plants grow next to bushy ones. Sharp angles are balanced by gentle bends. Any stream should be as natural as possible, moving from the east, going underground and flowing into the 'ocean' at the west. A stylised form of well head symbolises freshness.

❀ Some Japanese gardens have no water but are made up simply of rocks and gravel. This is because in the 15th century the Japanese Civil War put a stop to all gardening except in Buddhist monasteries. Here the monks kept up the tradition but in a very simple form. Sand represented the ocean and was raked daily to create wave forms. Uncut and weathered stones represented gods, mountains and animals.

The boundaries

❀ Japanese gardens are always separated from the surrounding land. Bamboo can be used for boundary fencing and for fencing to divide various parts of the garden. It should be tall and solid enough to conceal distracting views when contemplating the stones. Stepping stones laid on gravel are deliberately spaced to slow you down and allow you to leave your daily cares behind you as you walk.

❀ A typical feature of Japanese gardens is a small bamboo pipe which is pivoted on a stand. When the pipe is filled with water, it tips forward and then drops back on to a 'sounding stone' with a resonant clack. This device was originally designed as a bird and animal scarer to protect crops but acts as an interesting focal point in a modern Japanese garden.

BELOW: *Simplicity is the hallmark of a Japanese-style garden, as is retaining the spirit of the place. If there are old trees or rocks, try to retain them in your design. Gravel with stepping stones, a regularly shaped pond and characteristic plants such as bamboo and cherry trees are all within the spirit of the style.*

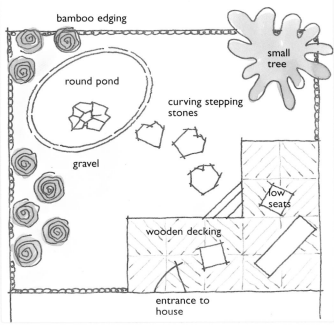

bamboo edging

round pond

gravel

small tree

curving stepping stones

low seats

wooden decking

entrance to house

THE TEA HOUSE GARDEN

IT IS thought that the Zen monk Muratushuko (1422–1502) probably originated the tea ceremony. He built a little tea hut in the middle of Kyoto, furnished with simple utensils, and this idea of simplicity and austerity caught on. The main feature of a tea house garden is the path of rough stepping stones preventing the visitor from trampling on the beautiful moss. Stone lanterns light the way at night and a stone bowl stands outside the tea house for cleaning the visitor spiritually and physically before entering the house.

❁ The tea house itself should resemble a small rustic retreat and was based on the traditional Japanese farmhouse. Traditionally, there should be no windows in this little house because there should be no view of the garden from inside. There might be a veranda, from which the shape of the garden can be viewed.

❁ The whole garden is in muted colours with plenty of moss, kept damp and green by watering, sprinkled on paths and stepping stones. Everything should appear totally natural. If there is a pond, it should be sinuous with jutting peninsulas and deep inlets, often shored up with rocks so that you can get a dramatic overview from the tea house veranda. Shrubs and bushes are clipped into shapes suggestive of mountains.

BELOW: *Although appearing to be informal, this is in fact a very formal garden, planted with the utmost discipline so that everything balances and is reflected in the pool.*

ABOVE: *Rocks are essential to a Japanese garden. They are chosen and placed with the greatest care and balanced by both the planting and other objects in the garden.*

THE STROLLING GARDEN

THIS is basically a garden walk in which visitors are taken around a deliberately designed pathway so as to see the various changing vistas and set views designed for that purpose. Artificial hills, artificial ponds, broad winding streams and waterfalls with islands, rocks and topiary emphasise the rustic ideal. There are paths and bridges in great number and variety, with a tea garden tucked away in a small separate garden within the strolling garden.

❀ Bridges can take several forms. The steep bridge is arched and usually painted red and black, but bridges are often simple planks laid across a narrow stretch of water. There may be stepping stones across the water as well as in the gravel or moss. Typically, both plants and rocks are rounded bun shapes and vertical elements are provided by trees. The ponds are full of golden carp.

❀ The gateway to the strolling garden is a pergola-like structure with a roof. The whole garden is dotted with trained and shaped conifers and miniature conifers. Ponds have many rocks and grass right up to the edges. This sort of strolling garden can be bounded by bamboo screens or it can merge gradually into natural woodland. Clipped paths and interestingly shaped rocks can show up to advantage against a white-painted wall.

BELOW: *This gravel garden represents the ocean with green islands floating in it. Such disciplined raked patterns are meant to be seen, rather like the parterre, from a window above that looks down on the garden.*

THE DRY GARDEN

THE dry landscape garden can represent a pond or the ocean and is often raked into wave-like patterns. It can look very stylish simply with cherry blossom hanging over it in spring. This sort of garden can be the answer to a small front garden overhung by trees where little will grow and which is more of a viewing garden than a garden to go into. This means the gravel will remain undisturbed and continue to look good for an appreciable length of time. Rocks can be set into the gravel and perhaps a dwarf pine tree such as *Pinus mugo* 'Mops' or an ornamental cherry.

SUITABLE PLANTS FOR JAPANESE-STYLE GARDENS

THE range of trees and flowers is fairly limited. If plants were used the main idea is to make the most of the different seasons. Pine trees, cherries and plums have a special place. Bamboo is an obvious choice of plant, being both natural looking and architectural. *Prunus* x *yedoensis* 'Shidare Yoshino' is a weeping cherry with pink buds ageing to pure white in short racemes. It grows to 4 m (13 ft) in 10 years. *Acer palmatum* 'Dissectum' forms a mound with arching shoots and has finely cut leaves turning gold in autumn. It will grow to 1.8 x 3 m (6 x 10 ft).

EXOTIC GARDENS

❧

**The exotic can be achieved simply by creating the effect of something foreign.
The Victorians were fascinated by foreign ideas and had gardens inspired by
many different countries. The nineteenth-century garden at Biddulph Grange
in Staffordshire – now owned by the National Trust and restored to its
original splendour – was designed in separate compartments, reflecting styles
of different parts of the world, including a Chinese garden, an Egyptian garden
with sphinxes and a Japanese garden.**

TROPICAL-LOOKING PLANTS
AND CONSERVATORIES

THE Victorians also used tropical-looking plants
which had to be taken into conservatories in the
winter in their summer borders. No truly tropical plant
will survive outside in temperate climates but recent
technological advances in propagation have produced a
number of tropical-looking plants, which can tolerate a
temperate climate even in winter. This gives tremendous
scope for creating exotic, jungly gardens, especially in
milder areas or in cities where the temperature is always
several degrees higher than in the areas surrounding them.

❀ Conservatories expand the possibilities, too, and even
the smallest one offers opportunities for creating really
flamboyant effects with climbing plants, hanging
baskets and epiphytic plants (those that grow on
other plants) hanging from branches, as well as
orchids and bromeliads.

ABOVE: *The stately yucca always surprises with its tall spire of white bells in
summer. It has a good architectural quality and will provide height in a border
or stand on its own.*

LEFT: *Bananas and canna lilies are truly exotic and the robinia tree behind
them has an exotic look as well. They will all grow in sheltered spots in
temperate areas, although you cannot expect the bananas to fruit.*

Creating a hardy jungle

❀ A jungle is lush with foliage, with many large, differently shaped leaves growing at different heights in
curtains of green, all overlapping and intertwining.
You can create this effect in the garden by using
vigorous climbers in association with large-leaved
hardy plants. Many plants grow very tall in the jungle,

ABOVE: *A lush and exotic water garden with a small walkway across the stream is positively tropical in feel.*

climbing up into the trees towards the light. You can simulate the height of a forest canopy by installing tall scaffolding screens. Make sure the scaffolding is robust and firmly fixed because many plants become very heavy when in leaf and need strong supports.

❀ If the site is sunny, the golden hop (*Humulus lupulus* 'Aureus') is a good candidate and perfectly hardy. Any vigorous climber with large leaves will add to the effect. The crimson glory vine (*Vitis coignetiae*) will eventually grow to 24 m (80 ft) and Virginia creeper to 15 m (50 ft). The leaves of both plants turn bright red in autumn. The evergreen *Clematis armandii* is another vigorous climber with plenty of large shiny leaves and will make your screen look like a snowstorm in spring with its masses of white flowers. For a shady site, *Hydrangea petiolaris* is a vigorous, hardy climber with handsome, flat, white lace-cap flower heads, which will reach 3.5 m (12 ft) on a wall or 5 m (16 ft) growing up a tree.

❀ For lower plants use *Fatsia japonica*, with its enormous palm-shaped leaves, or phormiums and yuccas. *Yucca glauca* is a mass of straight, thin grey-blue leaves 1.5 m (5 ft) across. Plant it in drifts close together. *Yucca* 'Vittorio Emmanuel II' is one of the biggest and best. It will grow to 1.8 m (6 ft).

RIGHT: *This small, sheltered garden relies on a few architectural and semi-tropical plants to give an exotic quality, using sculptural shapes and gaudy colours. Tall scaffolding provides a screen for vigorous climbers such as Virginia creeper, creating a jungle-like enclosed feeling. Palms, yuccas and large-leaved shrubs add to the jungle quality and a fountain provides sparkle and life.*

❀ For a moist site choose *Gunnera magellanica*, *Zantedeschia aethiopica* and *Rodgersia aesculifolia*. Bamboos are easy to grow and can contribute to the exotic feel of a garden. Choose ones that will not spread, or grow them where you really want a jungle or keep them in pots. *Phyllostachys aurea* is well behaved and will grow to 4.5 m (15 ft).

Creating a tender jungle

❀ Many tropical-looking plants, often from Mediterranean areas, although difficult to propagate, are not difficult to grow. Some prefer an exposed site; others grow best in dappled shade. The hardier eucalypts and the holm oak (*Quercus ilex*) are dense enough to keep the heat in and sparse enough to let light through, especially if you cut off their lower branches. *Eucalyptus aggregata*, *E. perriniana* and *E. parvifolia* all make good canopy trees.

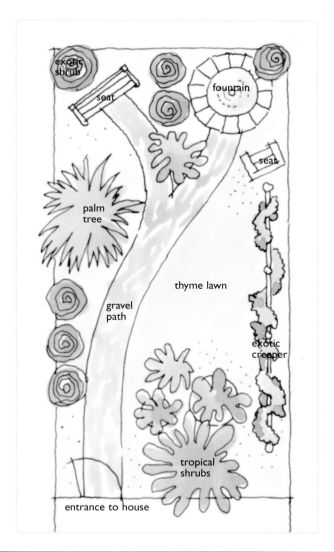

INDEX